D1560433

COOKIN' WITH THE LION

A Pinch of Blue, A Dash of White

A collection of recipes from
Alumni and Friends of Penn State
compiled by the
Penn State Alumni Association
University Park, PA

For additional copies of COOKIN' WITH THE LION please write:

Penn State Alumni Association
105 Old Main
University Park, PA 16802

First Edition, 15,000 copies, August 1988

Printed in the United States

Hart Graphics, Inc., Austin, Texas

Copyright© 1988

Penn State Alumni Association

Library of Congress 88-61553

ISBN 0-9620696-0-4

Cookin' With The Lion Committee

CO-CHAIRMEN . . . . Cathy Willigerod Dove '69
Susan Beck Wilson '71

FACULTY COORDINATOR . . . . Martha (Marty) Lewis Starling '66g, '69g
PROJECT COORDINATOR . . . . Lori Smith Baney
PROOF COORDINATOR . . . . Sandra L. Rothwell
SECRETARY . . . . Kimberly Pederson Murphy '85
STAFF ADVISOR . . . . Marjory Brubaker Sente '73

SPECIAL EDITORS
    Creative. Laura Lazarchik Jones '83
    Gracious Living . . . . Marcia Michalski Wharton '63
    Nutrition . . . . Amy Shetter Shuman '69

CATEGORY CHAIRMEN
    Appetizers/Beverages . . . . Beverly Evans
    Soups/Sandwiches . . . . Herbert C. Graves '50
                                            Nancy Greenwalt Graves '50
    Eggs and Dairy . . . . Patricia Marchezak McMurray '71
    Entrees . . . . Natalie Dabich Bailey '69
    Salads/Vegetables/Side Dishes . . . . Janet Woolever Raytek '65
    Breads/Pasta . . . . R. Evelyn Replogle Saubel '35
    Desserts. Marie Vergis Ferguson '69
    Tailgating . . . . Susan Young Henning '62

FIELD CHAIRMEN
    Nancy L. Coyne '77
    Judi Stern Feldstein
    Audrey Ann Glass '83
    Bert Douthett Goerder '41
    Debra Przywara McRae '81
    Kathleen A. Rittner '69, '72g

MEMBERS AT LARGE
    Peter L. Bordi Jr. '76, '81g
    Helen Skade Hintz '60
    Jonelle Jordan, '87 Honorary Alumna
    Judith Auritt Klein '47
    Jane Clarke Wettstone '67

PHOTOGRAPHERS
    M. Scott Johnson
    Dave Mengle

ILLUSTRATOR
    Michael Chesworth

3

Contributors

The cookbook committee thanks the hundreds of Penn Staters and friends of Penn State who contributed to **Cookin' With The Lion**. Many submitted their favorite recipes, others tested them, and still others entered the cookbook title contest. The committee selected Candace J. Vallimont's "A Pinch of Blue, A Dash of White" as the best entry in the cookbook-naming contest. So, we incorporated her suggestion with our working title for the final distinctive **Cookin' With The Lion — A Pinch of Blue, A Dash of White**.

Hall F. Achenbach '30
Charles T. Adomshick '59
Marie Adomshick
Thomas H. Ainsworth Jr. '41
Barbara Herscher Alberts '67
Wendy Leyfert Allen '82
David Carlson Allingham
Patricia Allingham-Carlson '78
Antoinette (Tonie) Leisey Allsopp '82
Virginia F. Althouse
Edward Anchel '60
Judith Kaplan Anchel
Lynette M. Anderson '80
Sheryl Flynn Antonenko '77
Ronald L. Applbaum '69g
Susan Stone Applbaum '68g
Janice P. Archibald '74, '85g
Robert A. Arnold '56
Leslie Asbury
Sharon Au
Connie Coates Ault '61
Lester (Les) F. Aungst Jr. '61g, '65g
Roberta (Bobbi) Binder Aungst '66g
Viv Auritt
Davies Uhler Bahr
Jean Nigh Bailey '60
Michael S. Bailey '64
Natalie Dabich Bailey '69
Benjamin J. Baker '73
Carmelyn Baker
Martha Tomasch Baker '74
Martin L. Baker '81
Michelle Stewart Baker '81
Cynthia Ackron Baldwin '66, '74g
Lori Smith Baney
James A. Bardi '69, '75g
Cheryl Polizzi Barrett '80g
Alvin L. Barth Jr. '58
Bonnie J. Barton '79g
Bruce E. Bayuk '51
JoAnne Johnson Beach '77
Patricia B. Beam
Robert E. Beam '48
Frances L. Bechdel
Wayne R. Bechdel '43
Joanne L. Beck '79
Joseph P. Beddia '71
Joanne Bauer Belfield '51
Robert S. Bell '36
Hobart E. Benchoff '54g
Bette A. Bender '77
Richard A. Benefield '48
Kim Benton-Crawford '82
Martin Berkowitz '51
Marguerite Yevitz Bernheim '81g
Darlene Betar
Walter H. Betar '56
Patricia Foley Bevers '70
Mark J. Bianchi '84
Diane E. Black '79

Laura A. Blackburn '85
John C. Blanda '69
Terry Dechert Blanda
Charles Blauser
Scott E. Bleggi '78
Bonita (Bonnie) Koch Bleiler '74
Katherine (Lani) Clark Bloomer '67, '76g
Donald W. Bogart Jr. '69
Judy Graham Bogart
Peter L. Bordi Jr. '76, '81g
Gail Bonnett Borio '70
Mary Timko Boris
Anna J. Borland
Esther Spence Bosnik '46
Carol A. Bouchard '87
Albert H. Bowers
Carol Schweinerbraten Bowers '61
Mary Lea Bowers
Jan M. Bowman '69
Shirley Bowman
Christine Young Boyer '68
William A. Bradley '31
Robert L. Branyan
David J. Braun '70
Elsie L. Brebner
Beth A. Brestensky '87
Sue Brewer
William M. Briggs Jr. '65, '69g
Ted Brown
Marc A. Brownstein '81
Judith Stout Brumbaugh '61
Anna Stafford Buffington '67
George R. Bundy '65
John J. Burich '73
Joyce V. Burich
Marjorie Harris Burns '58
H. Joan Lash Bush '59
Susan L. Bush '87
John I. Bushey
Betty Buss
C. Raymond Buss Jr. '51, '59g
Constance E. Butler '82
Theodore K. Byers '43
M. Jane Thurston Caldwell '61
Kimberlee S. Calviero '87
Marylin Camise
Cathy Mix Campbell '83
Louise Will Campbell '32
Maryellen B. Cannon '72
Susan A. Cardellino '75g
Karen Nelson Carey '63
Karen M. Carnabucci '73
Kris S. Carrara '83
Tammy Carrara
Helen Dobbins Casey
Samuel B. Casey Jr. '50
Joseph L. Cavinato '75g
Cherry Schrock Cerminara '71
John O. Chernega '80
Elaine Christmas

William G. Christmas '48
Sarann Delahanty Chubarov '79
David M. Ciscon '80
Mary Lotito Claire '57
Thomas (Thom) W. Clapper '65, '81g
Bess Treager Clarke '40
Donna Symmonds Clemson '55
Nancy Jacobs Collom '78
Darrell J. Colpo '75
Lois Bredholt Colpo '75g
Carolyn Williams Conrad '69
Michael C. Conti '79
Julian A. Cook Jr. '52
Mary Holes Correa '81
Deborah Suggars Costantino '76
Margaret (Peggy) A. Costello '74
Vicki Schneider Cousley '79
Lois Lunn Cowan '45, '72g
Nancy L. Coyne '77
Phyllis Watkins Crabtree '43, '68g
Debra Cannon Cramer '81
John W. Cramer Jr. '79
Patti Creghan-Ciuffetelli '79, '82
Marilyn J. Crowell '60
Thomas M. Dabich '73
Dean G. Damin '71
Betty Davis
Deborah Dean
Joyce Koch Deem '70
Linda Sakal Deichert '78
Kelley Davies Delaney '81
Alexander M. DellaBella III '80
Marcia Sanzotto DellaBella '82
Sharon L. DePalma '84
Kathryn Werst Detwiler '74g
Tonya C. DeVecchis '79
Arlene Gaffney Devereaux '72g
Susan Glenn DiBartolo '81
Betty H. Dileanis
Leonard P. Dileanis '48
Charlotte Lowe Dixon '41
Abby L. Dochat '86
Patricia Conrad Donohoe '68
Yvonne (Dolly) Fino Donovan '55
Craig R. Dorey '85
Robin L. Dorey
Beverly Dorman
Nancy Fry Doutt '51
Cathy Willigerod Dove '69
Louisa Drill
Martha Tobias Driver '42
Beth Orcutt Drude '80, '83g
William A. Dubas '85
Jane Fernsler Duncan '36
Ann Dunlap
Susan G. Dunlap '86
Sarabell (Kip) Shirm Dunlap '40
Diana R. Dunn '70g
Mark L. Eakman '80
Dennis J. Ebeling '73

4

Karen A. Ebeling
Helen W. Ebersole
Linda Brinsley Ebert '61
Louis M. Eble Jr. '48
Jean Eggert
Angela Eichenmiller
Marci Mayer Eisen '79
Martine Ehart Eisenberg '75, '77g
Stuart Eisenberg '75
Kathryn E. Elkins '70
Tonya Huber Emeigh '82, '85g
Robert D. Emrick '63
Sanford (Sandy) D. Engber '58
Ela Vardha Engineer '69g
Elizabeth A. Ennis '86g
Christel Ertel-Kahlbaugh '82
Beverly Evans
Diane Evans
Ralph B. Evans '57
Josephine Eyer
John P. Fadden '70
Mary Diehl Failor '42
Rosemary Faix
Andrea C. Falk '79
Cathy Bortz Fasnacht '81
Marcia Hutter Fehl '74g
Jay H. Feldstein '59
Judi Stern Feldstein
Rosella (Suzy) Katz Fenton '49
Lois G. Ferguson '86
Cornelia C. Ferguson
Marie Vergis Ferguson '69
T. Reed Ferguson Jr. '36
Heidi Hafer Ferrar '74, '76g, '78g
Rosanne Mellert Ferris '72
Michael D. Ferugio '87
Linda Fesmire
Louise Keefer Fisher '63
Margaret Roesner Fisher '81
Ruth E. Fisher
Joanne Fishman '75
Cheryl J. Flegle
Carissa L. Flesher
Meg Flipse
Helen Floruss
Kristina Volpe Focht '82
Lynn Fissinger Fogarty '67
Ronald P. Fogarty '66
Dorothy (Dot) Forrey
William C. Forrey '53, '71g
LaRue (Dana) Herwick Forwood '68
Ellen Miller Foster '49
Joyce Fox
Kenneth H. Franklin '65
Darlene Martz Fraser
David O. Fraser '64
Mariam (Mims) Fredman
George G. French '60
Helen Sevel Friedman '42
Konrad Fritz
Lydia Fritz
Ann Fullmer
Carole H. Gabauer '86
Samuel G. Gallu '40
Glenn W. Gamble '51, '55g, '59g
Mary Tilbrook Gamble '38
Nancy Saylor Gamble '52, '55g
Karen Bruno Ganter '71, '79g
Regina Kearney Garvey '74
Martha (Marty) Whipple Gasche
Kay Greb Gasowski '72
Mary Gates
Frances Inman Gaylord '34, '61g
Jane Gearhart
Sallie A. Geary '86
Patricia J. Geist
Edward W. George '45
Marian O. George
Nancy Scholz Geyer '70
Barbara E. Gillis
George Gillis '68
Kathleen A. Gilvary '82

Elaine F. Given
Hermine Gladstone
Lucy Raudabaugh Gnazzo '83
Bertha (Bert) Douthett Goerder '41
Norma Lash Goff '48
Ivalou Gunsallus Goldy
Mary Goodwin
Barbara Gordon
Carol Graham
Debra A. Graham '74
John R. Graham '64, '65g
Susan Johannesmeyer Grand '76
JoAnn Amato Grap '84
Rosanne Gonzales Grapsy '58
Norma Walker Gras '61g, '68g
Herbert C. Graves III, '50
Nancy Greenwalt Graves '50
Joseph F. Gray '48
Judith Reid Green '61
Marlene Greenberg
Michael A. Greenberg '69
Sandra Murdock Greene '66
Michael L. Greenwald '63
Anne Nelson Gregory '47
Louise Gregory-Pompa '82
Linda Leiner Gulick '80
Mary E. Gundel '46, '53g
Geraldine Dalio Haas '56
Karen Lacy Haas '75
Sandra Garo Haffner '78
Katherine (Kaye) Moore Hall '64
Nancy C. Hall '87
Martha Hallstrom
Julie Savelli Hallstrom
Robert M. Hallstrom '77
Alvira Konopka Hamill '41
Margaret Hardy
Lucille Rothschild Harris '40
Martha Worthington Harris '54
Marybelle Crossman Harris '41
Joanne Wagner Haskell '51
John A. Hauptman '49
James A. Haworth
Ellen Fisher Heaney '72
Dolores Rysak Heasley
Gale Wright Heavner '76
Elizabeth Fabian Heeney '52
Charlotte (Candy) Warfield Heidt '67
Joseph P. Heidt Jr.
George T. Henning '63
Susan Young Henning '62
Anna Cimmons Herbst '63
Gerald L. Hess '66
Jane Barber Hickman '80
Gary L. Hicks '82
Kathi A. Hicks
Gary K. Himes '60, '61g
Glenda Hinter Himes '60g
Helen Skade Hintz '60
Alice C. Hipple
G. Magdalene Hitchcock '26
Mariana Agnew Hoffman '57
Donald E. Hoke '58
Jean N. Hoke
Jackie Holland
Susan K. Holland '58
Lynne Oberson Holsopple '82
Lenore Kreiser Holt '80
Mrs. George Homich
Linda Hoover
Joseph A. Horn '80
Frederick J. Horne Jr. '38
Lou Horne
Mildred L. Horst
Mark G. Hoskinson '78
Cindy Schmucker Hower '81
Dorothy Foehr Huck '43
Carolyn L. Hughey '82
Shelvia Hummel
Barbara Black Huster
Dwight A. Huster '75g
Douglas E. Hutchinson '60

Carin Charters Illig '86
Herman D. Imber '39
Phyllis S. Imber
Barbara J. Inghram '81
Susan Loadman Ingram '75
Dorothy Intrieri
Barbara Gomber Isham '61
Gerard F. Jackson '67
Laura Danser Jackson '77
Mary McMaster Jackson '71
Sarah J. Jackson '42
Honora (Honey) Jaffe
Ingrid F. James
Jeanette Olach Janota '64g, '86g
Richard W. Jantzer '63
Andrew G. Jaros '54
Margaret Jaros
Jacquelyn Wengert Jenkins '49
Mrs. A. Dixon Johnson
Melinda Johnson
Meredith Johnson
John H. Jones Jr. '74, '77g
Laura Lazarchik Jones '83
Veronica Gambone Jones '73, '77g
Jonelle L. Jordan '87 Honorary Alumna
Barbara Frederick Junker '57
Gwen E. Kaufman '81
Eileen Keesey
Terry F. Keesey '69
Joyce Yundt Keiser '50
Lyn Kell
Donna Price Keller '69
Jayne Rider Kelly '68
Lyn Kennedy
Helen Luke Kenworthy '76g
Michelle R. Keslar '79
Kessey Stayer Kieselhorst '73
Preston King '67
Gail Kipp
Stephen K. Kipp '78
Carolyn Rice Kirkpatrick '49
Henry H. Kirkpatrick Jr. '48
Judith Auritt Klein '47
Robert Klein '48
Jane Beeghley Kline '55
Nancy Metro Klink '71
Jane Knepper
Joan Lentz Knepper '70
William D. Knepper '70
Susan Henry Knisley '78
Beverly Meyers Kocak
Nancy Kauchack Kochosky '59
Barbara Koebley
Bertha Koelzer
Mardelle Sacco Kopnicky '64
Jayne Koskinas
Desia Maso Kowalysko '79, '82g
Virginia (Ginny) Stumbaugh Krenzer '80
Judy Norton Krischker '61
Gerald (Jerry) T. Krivda '79
Jeanne Krochalis
Clair R. Krone '57, '61g
Patricia Rutland Krone
Dale A. Krug '80, '81g
Cecelia (Cece) Sacco Krumrine '68
Willis E. Kuhns '57, '61
Evelyn Papasavas Kurianowicz '76
Margaret A. Kuss '81
Mary Jane Winiarski Laquer '78
Christine McElroy Larson '84
Kenneth Larson
Warren T. Lash '88
Carol Strong Lauck '55
Donald G. Lauck Jr. '54
Georgeann Laughman '82
Amy Waugaman LaVelle '74
James A. Leamer Jr. '51
Gregory E. Lecker '87
Shirley M. LeFrancois '86
Cleta K. Leinbach
Richard B. Leinbach '57g, '78g
Elizabeth Brewer Lengle '81g

Marlene M. Leslie '79
Jeannine Bell LeVan '52
Margaret (Peggy) Seitz Liedtke '82
John M. Lilley
Alice Raphel Linberg '78g
Lois Lively
Patricia E. Loadman
Louise Inserra Lockwood '50
John S. Loeber '39
Deborah Diehl Loeffler
Stephen R. Loeffler '68
Gwendolyn B. Logan
John S. Logan '56
Valerie C. Lorenz '75, '78g
Gail Lowe
Mary Ellen Dunn Lowe '76
Kathleen Lorence Lucci '77
Lois Bellmeyer Lynch '62
Stephen P. Lyon '75
Anita E. Lyons
M. Jane Grubb Lysinger '53
Sandra Sabol MacDonald '69
Marion Lewis MacKinnon '48
Janet Madway
Huberta Young Manning '58
Eileen Bershok Marder '70
Janet T. Markle '76, '78g
Kim Marshall '79
Jean McNeil Martin '63
Kathie Martin
Robert L. Martin '87
Lori Martz
Joyce Leigh Mason
George A. Mastroianni '57
Nancy Brebner Mastroianni '57
James G. Matakovich '73
Lynda Saubel Matakovich '67
Ronald E. Matlack '67
Bonnie Pierce Matusik '83
Pamela Meyer May '77
Sheryl J. May '80
Donald S. Mayes '87
Sharon E. Maynard '80
James H. McCoy '71
Linda Koelzer McCoy '71
Stella McCoy
Harriet Wenner McGeehan '30
Timothy P. McGinley '82
Robin McKee
Susan Rode McLaughlin '72
Marna Ayers McLendon '72
Carol Braun McLoughlin '58
Robert G. McMillen '77
Patricia Marchezak McMurray '71
Maude McNaughton
Debra Przywara McRae '81
Andrea Somosky Meier
Louis H. Meier '73
Patrice L. Melcher '81
Linda Meluskey-Kriner '76
Terri L. Mentzer '84
Jean C. Meredith
Carole Ruff Merkel '58
Blanche J. Metzgar '86
Joan Burlein Michelotti '51
Robert M. Mihalek '87
Leona A. Mihalko '71, '81g
Craig J. Miller '70, '75g
Deborah DeMarco Miller '74
Helen Berkheimer Miller '85
Lidie von Zech Miller '30
Lorrie L. Miller
M. Jane Lauster Miller '58
Rebecca Deppen Miller '76
Tina Loshbough Miller '74
Karen J. Miller-McMillen '78
Pamela Miller-Weinberg '78
Theresa M. Milore '86
Marion Hall Mitchell '49
Sally McKeehen Mitchell '78
Sharon M. Mlodoch '77
Sandra Weiss Mock '63

June Daniels Mohan '45
Jeanette Ritter Mohnkern '29, '30g
Sheila Campbell Monastero '81
Marci Jo Mongeau '87
Linda Lieberman Monticciolo '79
May-Fay Easley Moore '64
Patricia Guasconi Moorhead '63
Judith R. Morgan
Kathleen Radabaugh Morris '76
Mary A. Morris '87
Nancy Bollenbacher Morrow '60
Susan Schulman Moss '66
Carol Hollinger Moyer '76
Kimberly Pederson Murphy '85
Violet Carver Murphy '58g
Louise Stroud Murray '55
Char Myers
Darwina L. Neal '65
Diana Lynn Neil
Larry W. Neil '77
Kristina Lyn New '86
Jane E. Nichols '66
Marta-Jo Prinkey Nicol '74
Anita Ankney Nolan '79
Madeline Pecora Nugent '70, '71g
Janet Cmiel Nuhfer '73
Gloria Oberlin
Eloise J. O'Brien '82
Margaret M. O'Brien
Nancy M. O'Connor
Colleen O'Donnell O'Mara '83
Janet Heeney O'Regan '77
Barbara A. O'Reilly '72g
John W. Oswald '73 Honorary Alumnus
Rosanel Owen Oswald '73 Honorary
  Alumna
Patricia Owens-Phillips '82
Emory C. Oyler '79
Janet L. Palamone '82
Doris Mawhinney Palzer '47
Faye H. Parmer
Thomas V. Pastorius '71g
Suzanne Pohland Paterno '61
Jon E. Pearson '68
Marian D. Peleski '67
Penn State Food Services
Pennsylvania Dairy Association
Jean Craumer Persson '47
Kathy DeVivo Pesta '79
Pat Peters
Lynn Petnick
Kathryn A. Petrich-LaFevre '82
Mary O'Connor Pfahl '40
Carol Salerno Pfeiffer '61
Nancy Phillips
Roman J. Pienta '54
Peggy Pierson
Jacki Pillot
Anne Curry Piper '52
B. Virginia Drayton Pirmann '74
W. Scott Pirmann III '71, '73g
Linda Plozner
E. Miriam Coder Podgorski '48g
Edward Podgorski
Michael S. Poerksen '85
Brian L. Polk '76
Lisa K. Pollisino '85
Louis F. Prato '59
Linda Camise Pratzman '77
L. Jean Hofmeister Purdy '40
James D. Pyles '87
Gregory J. Radio '69, '73g
Rosalie A. Radio
Maurice P. Ranc Jr. '61
Susan Rattenbury '89
Jami Rauch
James J. Raytek '65, '67g
Janet Woolever Raytek '65
Alex O. Reethof '80
Robert P. Rehkopf '50
Jeffrey R. Reiche '79
Frances Reidy

Sheila A. Reilly '66g
Barry B. Rein '62
Catherine Shultz Rein '64
Donald A. Remley '82
Jeanne Livingston Renton
William H. Renton '47
Elizabeth (Libby) Anstine Reynolds '67
Betty Hallowell Rhodes '67
Kathy Rhodes
Olive Brown Rice '39
Danielle Piacine Richards '80
Marge Richards
B. Gene Riechers Jr. '77
Douglas L. Risher '71
Terrie Heinrich Rizzo '68
Judith Colbeck Roberts '61
Mary Jane Dalton Roelofs '41
Rita Apter Rolter '49
Sandy Rosenbaum
Frances Dektor Rothman '53
Sandra L. Rothwell
Linda Friedrichs Rowan '78
Mark B. Rubin '81
Charlotte Harris Rudel '55
Barbara Edwards Rudisill '84g
Edwin S. Runkle '75
Brenda J. Ruth '84
Sharon Neff Ryba '80
Lucille Kreisman Safferman '54
Gloria J. Sakal '81
Celeste Sychterz Salvaggio '82
Denise Goff Sapolich '78
James F. Sarver '57, '58g, '61g
R. Evelyn Replogle Saubel '35
Rose (Ronnie) Schulman Saunders '45
Cathy Saverneno
Morton Schneider '39, '41g
Jacqueline L. Schoch '51, '60g, '65g
Marjorie Ganter Scholtz '62
Joan L. Schreyer
Helen Norris Schroeder '53
Donald M. Schuler '75
Connie Schulz
Schuylkill Campus
Linda Rubin Schwab
Morris M. Schwab '40
Jane Sciarrone
Jennifer Sciortino
Rosario C. Sciortino '79
Debra Brown Seamon '72
Kimberly S. Seman '81
Marjory Brubaker Sente '73
Mary Evans Serpento '76
Marye Hartzell Settles '51
Joan E. Sexton '81, '86g
Jill Wert Shadle '85
Mary Comfort Shannon '63
Janice Krauss Shapiro '74
Lynda Johnson Sheffer '73
Marion F. Shetter
Janet Meyers Shockey '72g
JoAnn Koch Shore '73, '75g
Diana Ciclamino Short '78g
Amy Shetter Shuman '69
John D. Shuman '77
Mary Dolier Shuman '36
Elissa M. Sichi
Harry J. Sichi '59
Judith O'Donnell Sieg '59
Mia M. Sieminski-Summe '72
Maryann Siler
Richard W. Sinclair '69
Jackie L. Singel
Mark S. Singel '74
Harry E. Slep IV '77
Larry Smarr
Paul D. Smeltzer Jr. '77
Barbara Smith
Candace A. Smith '77
Donna M. Smith '86
Mary A. Smith
Meta C. Smith

6

Nancy L. Smith
Maryann Snider
Jeanne Snyder
Mary K. Snyder '76
Kathryn M. Soderberg '86g
Frances Neidigh Sowko '50
Raymond C. Sowko '50
Bonnie Yeakel Spetzer
Kathleen L. Spicher '71, '76g, '84g
Barbara Morrison Stahl '46
C. Drew Stahl '47, '49g, '54g
M. Romayne Parks Stanell '50
Martha (Marty) Lewis Starling '66g, '69g
Christine L. Steele '86
Deanna Stegeman
Pamela A. Stein '83
Mona Steitman
Mary McMullen Stella '74
George K. Stennett '56
Sallie H. Stennett
Michele Bubser Stepler '81
Bernadette Heagney Stevenson '36
Kevin E. Still '83
Joan Hickerson Stoeckinger '57
Lura Stoedefalke
Jane R. Stoner
Grace Miller Stover '50
Ward M. Stover '51, '81g
Corinne Joy Strasmyer
Robert H. Strasmyer '39
Suzanne Finke Strickler '74
Phyllis Breisch Stuby '60, '69g
Patricia Turner Sulouff '60
Marianne Gushen Swade '78
Virginia Minshall Swartz '47, '51g, '85g
Janet Heinel Swenson '68
Charmasielle L. Swope
James G. Swope Jr. '60
Marian Barbey Tait '37
Louise C. Tarman
Joan Glasgow Theobald '68
Jean E. Thomson
Robert D. Thomson '51, '52g
William A. Thomson '46, '47g
James J. Tietjen '58g, '63g
Mary-Ellen Tietjen
Dorothy Todaro
Mario F. Todaro '57, '75g
Edward S. Tomezsko '61g, '62g
Lynnda M. Tomorie '78

Anne Miller Torda '61
Carolyn Spengler Tothero '55
Diane Freiermuth Travers '84
Penny L. Trick '74, '76g
Alice Morrow Trumbauer '59
Glenn R. Trumbull '76
Joyce Trigiano Turley-Nicholas '50
James J. Tusar '84
Bonnie Myers Tuten '69
Michelle Klemo Tyson '77
Stephanie Tyworth
Lori Bowers Uhazie '82
Doreen M. Ulichney '78
Anne D'Olier Ulmer '32, '66g
Robert C. Umbenhen Jr.
Natalie A. Updegrove '84
Margi Jacob Urquhart '71
Candace J. Vallimont '75
Gerald R. Van Akin '55
Ruth Stufft Van Akin '54
Harold A. Vanasse Jr. '87
James B. Vandergrift '64
Judy Vandergrift
Jo Vaughan
Diane Damweber Voit '72
Ronald K. Wackowski '80
Sally White Wackowski '80
Ellen Barber Waldeck '70g
Josephine Schmeiser Walker '86
    Honorary Alumna
Kay Walker
Mary K. Walker
William R. Walker '40
Tammi L. Walsh '82
Robert V. Waltemeyer '56
Alice Herr Walter '44
Ronald Q. Warren '76
Holly Deeslie Warrington '80
Scott C. Warrington '82, '83g
Marian Colver Wasel '48
Marguerite (Peggy) Scheaffer
    Washabaugh '40
Karen D. Watson '87
Susan Heidenwolf Weaver '80
Judy Holler Weber '77
Eleanor Strauss Weirman '58
Jean Weller
Diane K. Wendling '84
Robert S. Werba '72, '75g

Harry T. Werner '74
Linda Whitlock Werner
Eleanor K. Wettstone
Eugene Wettstone '79 Honorary
    Alumnus
Jane Clarke Wettstone '67
Jerry R. Wettstone '62, '63g
Marcia Michalski Wharton '63
Glennis R. Wheelock
Priscilla W. Wheelock
Sally Plasterer Whitney '74
Joan Yerger Williams '53, '85g
Nancy Williams
Beverly Wilson
Edward J. Wilson '70
Krista Wescoat Wilson '80
Susan Beck Wilson '71
Dorothy White Wingert '53
Adele Winston
Faith Szuhaj Wojtowicz '64
Paxton G. Wolfe '50
Kathleen Hammond Woodard '52
Dale E. Woomert '49, '51g
Sally T. Woomert
Patricia Wright
Constance (Connie) Sullivan Yake '81
Barbara Yingling
Debra K. Young '86
Joan Greiff Young '70
Joanne Devaux Young '53
Faith Gallagher Zamary '76
Charlotte Brown Zarfoss '64
Thomas F. Zarfoss '65
Kurt Zaspel Jr. '52
Wilma Zaspel
Catherine King Zernhelt '59
Francis L. Zernhelt '61
Elaine Bottino Ziegler '71
Alicia Peel Zilker '72, '76g
Anne Harvey Zimmerman '78
Will Zimmerman

The Penn State Clubs of:

Los Angeles
Cleveland
Detroit
Warren County, Pennsylvania
Washington, D.C.

In addition to the contributors already mentioned, the cookbook committee thanks
the Alumni Council, Alumni Association staff and numerous University employees
for all their help in the production of **Cookin' With The Lion**. In particular we wish
to thank:

Lauren Barner
Phyllis Belk
John S. Bischoff '57
William M. Bodnar '79
Jill Buzzell '88
Penny Hubler Carlson '81, '84g
David M. Ciscon '80
Donna Symmonds Clemson '55
Josephine Rider Chesworth '60
Richard H. Dorman '80g
Susan Luzier Fields
Susan Frandsen
Michael L. Greenwald '63
Brenda Grenoble

Pat Gunzerath
Gwen E. Kaufman '81
Fran Klinefelter
Beverley J. LaPorte
Andrew Milne '90
Dorothy Irwin Mitstifer '72g, '76g
Geraldine (Gerrie) Mills Murphy '68, '81
Francis (Frank) X. O'Brien '54
Thomas R. Palchak '80
Karen Piwonski '90
Robert K. Reese Jr. '74
William J. Rothwell
Evelyn Replogle Saubel '35

JoAnn Koch Shore '73, '75g
John D. Shuman '69
Kirsten Vensel '90
Linda Whitlock Werner
Jerry R. Wettstone '62, '63g
Elizabeth Klens Wilson '83g
Timothy D. Williams

HUB Catering
University House staff
Penn State Bakery
Penn State Bookstore
Penn State Creamery

Table of Contents

Tailgating

We are reminded continually that our Penn State experience is at once the same as that of others and yet unique.

Memories surface from as recently as last week's game or as long ago as the date on your diploma. We recall thousands of friendly faces, some of them very dear friends. As students we shared everything from the boxes of cookies sent from home to ice cream cones at the Creamery. We grabbed a bite at Allencrest in the '30s and '40s, and in later years devoured lasagna and cheese cake at the Tavern, stickies at the College Diner, and beer at the Skeller. We gobbled hot dogs at the stadium, popcorn in the suites, cold cider at the Hort Show and pizza in our rooms. In the dining halls we never missed a chance to eat any dieter's relinquished Midnight Cake or to complain about "mystery meat" with "all-purpose" gravy. We looked forward to parents' invitations to enjoy the ambience of Sunday dinner at the Nittany Lion Inn.

As alumni, our sharing continues, most visibly at the tailgates. Some have never been back for one of these extravaganzas but continue to share the spirit at home television parties using a tailgate theme. To duplicate the Beaver Stadium experience, tailgate from the trunk of your car parked in the driveway, rent portable bleachers to replace the furniture in your family room, turn off the heat, bundle up to keep warm, open the doors and let a few fall leaves blow inside.

Penn Staters are accomplished tailgaters. We've perfected the art of getting out of the kitchen and in with the crowd at the games. Whether we have days to prepare or very limited time, we have learned to "package" tailgates.

Some tailgates look like buffets taken right out of a magazine spread. These are usually put together by several friends who make it a joint effort. But you don't need to offer a great variety of food at a tailgate. A menu as simple as chips and veggies with dip or other finger foods is great for a tailgate.

Because of the wide range of tailgate possibilities, a selection of "Tailgate Recipes" exclusive from the other food categories is impossible. Instead you will find tailgate recipes throughout **Cookin' With The Lion**. Our Tailgating Lion will be your guide! Follow him through the book for the best tailgate recipes — from extravagant to simple.

Menu planning for tailgates emphasizes "portability" and foods that hold up to day-ahead preparation and night-after nibbling. There is also the freedom to include any kind of dish at all, just for the fun of it. One party included breaking open a fresh coconut!

To a tossed salad, add an already prepared casserole heated in one of those handy RVs or more likely warmed on a gas stove. Or plan a completely cold entree, such as Glazed Ham Loaf, and a vegetable medley. Add some crusty French rolls from your favorite bakery or an easy-to-make bread from your kitchen such as Poppy Seed French Bread or Oatmeal Wheat Bread. Attractive trays of fresh fruit and any of the sure-fire irresistible desserts included in these pages are tasty additions.

Anticipate a time crunch? Start early with some of our recipes earmarked for freezing so they're ready for the weekend. Or purchase deli sandwiches and present them in clear plastic bags or colorful cellophane tied with blue and white ribbons. Remember, too, that convenience foods and assorted prepared salads can augment many a tailgate.

Some tailgaters write or call in their food orders to eateries around town; then it's easy to pick up the food when they arrive. Other fans keep an eye out for delis or sandwich shops en route to the games and do their tailgate preparation with ease as they travel.

A theme cake added novelty and saved time for the hosts at one tailgate party. They featured a spectacular victory sheet cake, decorated with a lifelike navy blue replica of the Lion shrine with a wide navy blue border with football mums.

The hostess writes, "The cake drew a crowd of admirers and photographers . . . many in Irish green! We shared our cake with all, later finding that we had given old Notre Dame a big touch of Blue/White spirit. The intensity of the blue icing gave one and all blue teeth, lips, fingers and gums!"

Penn Staters know how to package a tailgate!

You have probably seen students holding balloons, standing around with purchased sandwiches and cans of soda for their tailgate. Others get together as groups to grill hamburgers, steaks and chicken. You have seen meals warming on Coleman stoves, great-looking tablecovers (such as quilts and bright woven rugs), floral centerpieces fashioned from a few of the blue and white pom poms and the traditional mum corsages, candelabra, champagne buckets, and all manner of seating arrangements! You may say that you would never do "all that." Yet, it takes no more time to pack an ice bucket with a bottle of wine or champagne than to fill a cooler with beer and soda. Use your individuality to package your tailgate. The fare can be simple or it can be fancy, but have some fun with the presentation.

Tailgating offers the widest freedom of choice in entertaining. It's having dishes, glasses and silverware that are both practical and fun to use such as the colorful array of paper, plastic and lucite pieces available today. It's poking around your home to find interesting serving pieces that might not necessarily be intended for use at the table. Consider using bright plaid acrylic (washable) scarves as runners for your table, laid down the center of your blanket, stretched across the back of your trunk as a backdrop, or tied around a big basket of fresh fruit for a colorful touch.

Containers of all sizes are indispensable for tailgating. Use oversized Penn State cans at both home and stadium tailgates to pack the whole picnic. The lid can double as an extra tray. Small decorative cans also make an appealing appearance. Try them! . . .

   . . . as personal containers for potato chips
   . . . for individual hors d' oeuvre "pots" packed with chilled raw
          vegetables
   . . . as "nibble-tins"
   . . . for wrapped portions of whole fresh fruits
   . . . as individual dessert cachepots

By using these or other interesting containers, you can store, transfer and serve in style.

Tailgate hosts often enjoy the spontaneous joy of including a few extra hungry Lions at the last moment . . . so be ready! Tuck in one more wedge of Penn State Creamery cheese and a box of crackers, a few extra pieces of fruit, an additional thermos of coffee, and a few more cookies. If you don't need them at the tailgate, you can always enjoy them for your private party on the drive home.

Tailgate Hints

One important consideration is weather. In the beginning of the season when it's warm, take the makings for cold sandwiches (hoagies — make your own). Also, stay away from candy at September games. It will melt quickly in the sun. During September avoid salads containing mayonnaise. Conversely, for November games plan foods that can be heated on a Coleman stove (charcoal grills are prohibited at the stadium). This is a good time for hot drinks, soups and main dishes (chili, sloppy joe's, ham barbecue).

Be creative in using heating space. Double boilers can heat two items at one time. You can use pan lids for heating some items. Take things that travel well. "Perfect" tailgate foods (for those who travel and need to prepare on Thursday or Friday) are those that need to marinate or sit for a few days before serving.

Be sure to take several trash bags to make cleanup easy.

Take a little extra to eat and offer to share. The kids selling items in the parking lots are usually glad for some home-cooked food. Be sure to comply with University regulations on alcohol and serve only soft drinks to minors.

Have a dining canopy in case of a sudden shower or at least have a piece of plastic to cover the food.

We also want you to meet our Lean Lion. He will be found throughout **Cookin' With The Lion** offering suggestions and recipe alterations for a healthier, more nutritious diet.

Appetizers/Beverages

Appetizers are dips, spreads, a round of Brie, raw or marinated vegetables, or individually prepared morsels. You name it, as just about anything can be sized to a finger food or at least adapted for a different look. Your favorite chicken recipe might turn out to be a super appetizer. Just mold bite-sized pieces of boneless breasts and make the same sauce. (Consider Chicken Nittany with Mushroom Sauce.) You'll have to adjust cooking times, but that should work out easily. Instead of rice with the main chicken course, serve thin slices of a sturdy bread with the chicken appetizers.

When you are preparing your favorite meatballs, reserve some of the mixture to form into smaller balls (a tiny ice cream scoop saves time); then freeze. Stir the frozen meatballs into heated sauce and cook covered until meatballs are heated through, about 15 minutes. Remember that you often can use the same meatball recipe with several different sauces.

You can adapt some of your favorite recipes for appetizers. It works the other way around, too. Many of your favorite appetizers would be delicious as a main course. Now, take those tiny meatballs, for example . . . make them larger for your main dish entree. The possibilities are endless.

A few tempting hors d'oeuvres or appetizers tucked securely in your freezer can be a bonus, too. In addition to using them as appetite teasers, they are often the main event for a cocktail buffet or reception. They are equally important as just the right accompaniment to a main course salad or a soup supper.

Remember when you could get a fresh (not the syrup) lemon coke for five cents at the Corner Room? Remember a little glass of "fruit shrub" — cranberry juice with a bit of sherbet served at the dress-up (heels and hose), holiday candlelight dinners in the dining halls? Remember the punch at college and sorority teas? The beer at fraternity parties?

How often did you grab a cup of coffee in the sandwich shop in the basement of Old Main? Did you ever dash into the HUB Eatery for a refreshing glass of iced tea to cool off during the Arts Festival? Everyone has different memories, but beverages signal a chance to relax, a time to enjoy each other.

How full is your recipe file marked "Beverages"? Many tasty drinks are commercially prepared, so it's easy to overlook other refreshing possibilities that you can make yourself. In this chapter, you can almost feel and see your Penn State friends offering you their favorite drinks!

Have some fun experimenting with a variety of shapes and sizes of glassware! Envision chunky frosted tumblers of Stately Slush; clear lucite wine glasses of Final Yard Fruit Punch; tall goblets of Mint Tea; and antique crystal punch cups of Strawberry Lemonade Punch. Presenting a drink to your family and guests in a really great glass or cup is fun and one of the pleasures of entertaining.

Also, experiment with different locations to create new memories! You are especially fortunate if you have your kitchen table by a window, or a few cozy chairs in the sunniest room in your home, or a shady tree with a cool haven on the grass beneath. Maybe you'll have a chance to return to one of your favorite old haunts in the shadow of Mt. Nittany. Find happy places to relax and share a refreshing beverage with someone special!

Hot Broccoli Dip

PREPARATION TIME: *40 minutes*
YIELD: *1 quart*

1 **(10 ounce) package frozen chopped broccoli**	1. Cook broccoli according to package directions and drain well.
½ **cup chopped onion**	2. Sauté onions, celery and mushrooms in butter until tender.
½ **cup chopped celery**	
½ **cup chopped mushrooms**	3. Combine broccoli, soup and cheese in medium saucepan. Cook over low heat until cheese melts, stirring occasionally.
3 **tablespoons melted butter**	
1 **(10½ ounce) can cream of mushroom soup**	4. Add sautéed vegetables to broccoli mixture, stirring well.
1 **(6 ounce) package garlic cheese, diced**	5. Serve hot! A chafing dish is a good idea. Serve with chips or vegetables to dip into this delicious combination.

Patricia E. Loadman

Fiesta Victory Dip

PREPARATION TIME: *1 hour 30 minutes*
YIELD: *2 quarts*

3 **large onions**	1. Grind onions and garlic in food chopper, but keep peppers separate and grind them last.
3 **cloves garlic**	
3 **(4 ounce) cans green chili peppers**	2. Brown onions and garlic in small amount of margarine first, then add peppers.
Margarine	
3 **(16 ounce) cans tomatoes**	3. Drain tomatoes (do not use any of the juice) and add to the above.
2 **pounds Velveeta cheese**	4. Simmer one hour.
Salt, to taste	5. Cut cheese in chunks. Add and cook until cheese is melted.
Corn chips or tortilla chips	6. Serve warm with chips.

Col. (Ret.) John S. Loeber '39 Journ

The Nittany Lion DU Dip

PREPARATION TIME: *35 minutes*
YIELD: *12 – 14 servings*

1 (8½ ounce) can artichoke hearts	1. Butter a 1 quart casserole and break up artichoke hearts into the casserole.
½ cup mayonnaise	
½ teaspoon garlic salt	2. Mix in the rest of the ingredients.
½ cup Parmesan cheese	3. Top with extra Parmesan cheese.
Parmesan cheese for topping	4. Bake at 350° for 20 minutes. Serve with crackers.

"This recipe goes back a few years. It was given to me by a teacher in Penn Hills where I taught. My husband is a 1951 graduate and a Delta Upsilon brother. We have used this recipe on many occasions with the DUs and Penn State Alumni."

Wilma Zaspel
Kurt Zaspel Jr. '52 Hort

Garlic powder can always be substituted for garlic salt, or use fresh garlic. Garlic presses are a wonderful addition to any kitchen.

Penn State Club of Greater L.A. Dip

PREPARATION TIME: *1 hour 30 minutes*

YIELD: *4 – 8 servings*

2 **round loaves of unsliced bread (farmer's or sheepherder's bread)**

6 **(3 ounce) packages cream cheese with chives**

1 **(2½ ounce) jar dried beef**

4 **green onions, chopped (including green part)**

1 **(7 ounce) can diced green chilies**

1. Slice top of one loaf of bread and set aside. Cut out inside of bread leaving a half inch shell

2. Soften cream cheese in microwave. Mix in dried beef, onions, and chilies. Fill one bread round with mixture. Place lid on top. Wrap in aluminum foil.

3. Bake at 350° for 1 hour.

4. Cut the remaining bread into 2-inch lengths. Serve with dip.

This can easily be heated in a glass dish and served with crackers if bread is not available.

Judy Graham Bogart
Donald W. Bogart Jr. '69 ME

Approximately 3,000 pounds of nachos are sold each Penn State home football game.

Lion Lovers' Hot Crab Dip

PREPARATION TIME: *1 hour 30 minutes*
YIELD: *12 – 16 servings*

3 (8 ounce) packages cream cheese

½ cup mayonnaise

¼ cup Miracle Whip

2 pounds fresh Alaskan king crab meat (do not use claw meat)

½ teaspoon garlic powder

2 teaspoons prepared dark mustard (not yellow, can be wine mustard)

¼ cup white wine (not cooking wine)

3 teaspoons powdered sugar

1 teaspoon onion juice (optional)

Salt and pepper to taste

2 – 3 bags corn chips

1. Melt cream cheese in top of double boiler or in microwave on defrost.

2. Add remaining ingredients and mix well.

3. Warm over low heat for about an hour to allow flavors to blend. Best when made the day before, chilled and then reheated.

4. Serve warm with corn chips.

DO NOT SKIMP ON THE CRAB — that is the true secret of the recipe!

Darlene Martz Fraser
David O. Fraser '64 EE

Crab Dip

PREPARATION TIME: *15 minutes plus 15 minutes heating time*
YIELD: *12 – 16 servings*

1 (6 – 7 ounce) can king crab

8 ounces cream cheese, softened

1 teaspoon horseradish

Milk (just enough to combine ingredients)

Pinch white pepper

2 teaspoons finely chopped onion

4 teaspoons finely chopped almonds

1. Stir all ingredients together except for almonds.

2. Pour into small casserole dish and sprinkle with almonds.

3. Heat at 300° for 15 minutes.

4. Serve on crackers.

Easy. Can double easily. Must serve immediately.

Rosanel Owen Oswald '73 Honorary Alumna
John W. Oswald '73 Honorary Alumnus

Lion Tamer Spinach Dip

PREPARATION TIME: *10 minutes*
YIELD: *2½ cups*

1 (10 ounce) box chopped spinach, thawed (squeeze all liquid out)

1 cup mayonnaise

1 cup sour cream

1 (1.4 ounce) package dry vegetable soup mix

1 (8 ounce) can chopped water chestnuts

1 round unsliced loaf of bread (rye is excellent)

1. Mix the first 5 ingredients together.

2. Hollow out the round loaf of bread by removing bite-size pieces from the center of the loaf and leaving a shell.

3. Fill the hollowed out center with the mixed ingredients.

4. Place the bread pieces around the loaf on a tray to be used for dipping.

Marion Hall Mitchell '49 HEc

Try using ½ cup mayonnaise, ½ cup sour cream and 1 cup non-fat yogurt to decrease the fat and calories.

Mt. Nittany Cheese Bowl

PREPARATION TIME: *45 minutes plus overnight chilling*

YIELD: *10 – 12 servings*

4 ounces fresh mushrooms, chopped

1 clove garlic, crushed

Chopped onion, to taste

¼ cup margarine

10 ounces sharp Cheddar cheese, shredded

1 tablespoon Worcestershire sauce

1 teaspoon dry mustard

½ cup light beer

8 ounces cream cheese

1 loaf round rye bread

1. Sauté mushrooms, garlic and onion in a skillet with melted margarine.

2. When tender add cheese, Worcestershire sauce, and dry mustard. Stir until cheese is melted.

3. Add beer and stir. Store this mixture in the refrigerator, overnight if possible. (This mixture may separate while stored, but the setting gives it a chance to blend all flavors.)

4. Before serving, blend cream cheese into mixture.

5. Hollow out the loaf of rye bread and fill with cheese mixture. Center of bread should be cut into cubes. Spread cheese on bread cubes.

Cherry Schrock Cerminara '71 FSHA

To decrease fat, use 5 ounces Cheddar and 5 ounces low-fat mozzarella cheese and substitute non-fat plain yogurt or creamed tofu for the cream cheese.

Dill Dip

PREPARATION TIME: *1 hour plus chilling time*

YIELD: *2½ cups*

1 cup mayonnaise

3 ounces cream cheese

1 tablespoon shredded fresh onion

1 teaspoon minced parsley

½ teaspoon Beau Monde seasoning

2 teaspoons dill weed

½ teaspoon curry powder

1 cup sour cream

Assorted vegetables: sliced cucumber, carrot sticks, green pepper sticks, celery sticks, whole mushrooms, broccoli and cauliflower flowerettes, cherry tomatoes, green olives, black pitted olives, zucchini sticks

Potato chips

Crackers

1. Combine and mix the mayonnaise, cream cheese, onion, parsley, Beau Monde, dill weed, curry powder and sour cream.

2. Chill in refrigerator.

3. Prepare vegetables and arrange on large platter. Or may be served with potato chips or crackers.

Marilyn J. Crowell '60 SecEd

Cream Cheese & Crab Meat Appetizer

PREPARATION TIME: *10 minutes*

YIELD: *2 cups*

1 (6 ounce) package king or snow crab meat

1 (8 ounce) package cream cheese

1 (12 ounce) bottle chili sauce

2 teaspoons horseradish

Juice of ½ lemon

1. Defrost and squeeze liquid from crab meat.

2. Place cream cheese on plate. Sprinkle crab meat over cream cheese block.

3. Mix chili sauce, horseradish and lemon juice together. Pour over crab meat.

4. Serve with assorted crackers.

Sallie H. Stennett
George K. Stennett '56 A&L

Mexican Nittany Salad

PREPARATION TIME: *15 minutes*
YIELD: *8 – 10 servings*

2 ripe avocados, peeled	1. In food processor combine peeled avocados and cream cheese.
8 ounces cream cheese	
½ head lettuce, cut in thin slices	2. Spread in a 9 × 9-inch square glass pan.
1 (8 ounce) jar green Spanish olives	3. Layer in the following order: the lettuce, olives, cheese, tomato and salsa. Refrigerate until ready to serve.
8 ounces grated sharp Cheddar cheese	
1 large tomato, diced	4. Just before serving top with a large spoonful of sour cream.
1 (12 ounce) jar mild salsa sauce	
Sour cream	5. Using corn chips, dig down to bottom and scoop up dip.
Corn chips	

Gail Bonnett Borio '70 EKEd

Pizza Dip

PREPARATION TIME: *20 – 30 minutes*
YIELD: *8 – 12 servings*

8 ounces whipped cream cheese	1. Spread cream cheese on a 12-inch round plate. Cover plate evenly.
¾ cup cocktail sauce	
1 (6 ounce) can shrimp, drained and rinsed	2. Spread cocktail sauce over cream cheese. Sprinkle shrimp over the cocktail sauce. Then layer pepperoni, mushrooms and olives. Sprinkle mozzarella cheese over the top. Serve with crackers for scooping.
4 ounces pepperoni, sliced thin and halved	
10 – 12 mushrooms, sliced	
1 small can black olives, sliced	
8 ounces mozzarella cheese, shredded	

Wendy Leyfert Allen '82 CmDis

Part-skim mozzarella cheese slightly decreases the fat.

Shrimp Appetizer

PREPARATION TIME: *20 minutes*
YIELD: *15 servings*

8 ounces cream cheese, softened

1 cup ketchup

2 tablespoons horseradish

1 teaspoon lemon juice

1 (6 ounce) can small shrimp

1 cup chopped green pepper

1 cup chopped tomatoes

3 scallions, sliced

½ cup sliced black olives

Shredded mozzarella cheese

Crackers or bagel chips

1. Spread cream cheese on a plate or platter.
2. Combine ketchup, horseradish, lemon juice and shrimp together.
3. Spread over cream cheese.
4. Sprinkle the green pepper, tomatoes, scallions, black olives and mozzarella cheese on top.
5. Serve with crackers or bagel chips.

Linda Koelzer McCoy '71 EKEd

Egg and Chili Appetizer

PREPARATION TIME: *10 minutes plus 20 minutes cooking time*
YIELD: *10 – 12 servings*

2 (4 ounce) cans chopped green chili peppers

½ – ¾ pound shredded Cheddar cheese

4 eggs, beaten

Corn chips

1. Grease an 8 × 8-inch baking dish.
2. Spread chilies on bottom of pan.
3. Spread cheese on top
4. Beat eggs and pour over top.
5. Bake at 350° for 20 minutes or until eggs are set.
6. Serve immediately, hot with corn chips.

Betty Hallowell Rhodes '67 PhEd

Taco Dip

PREPARATION TIME: *20 minutes*
YIELD: *8 – 10 servings*

16 ounces sour cream

8 ounces cream cheese

1 (1¼ ounce) package taco seasoning

2 cups shredded lettuce

3 green onions, chopped

8 ounces shredded Cheddar cheese

2 tomatoes, diced

Nacho chips

1. Mix sour cream, cream cheese and taco seasoning until smooth. Cover bottom of a deep pie dish.

2. Cover sour cream mixture with shredded lettuce and green onions.

3. Cover lettuce with Cheddar cheese.

4. Layer tomatoes over cheese.

5. Serve with nachos.

"Can do ahead and keep refrigerated. Great for tailgating parties."

Evelyn Papasavas Kurianowicz '76 HPE

Canteen food services sell approximately 8,000 cups of popcorn each Penn State home football game.

Fiesta Bowl Dip

PREPARATION TIME: *15 minutes*
YIELD: *10 servings*

3 **medium avocados, ripe and mashed**	1. Mix together mashed avocados, lemon juice, salt and pepper. Set aside.
2 **tablespoons lemon juice**	2. Mix together sour cream, mayonnaise and taco seasoning in separate bowl. Set aside.
½ **teaspoon salt**	
¼ **teaspoon pepper**	3. Spread bean dip on a large serving platter.
1 **cup sour cream**	
1 **cup mayonnaise**	4. Spread avocado mixture over bean dip, leaving a 1-inch border of bean dip.
1 **(1¼ ounce) package taco seasoning mix**	
2 **(10½ ounce) cans bean dip**	5. Spread taco seasoning mixture over avocado layer, leaving a 1-inch border of avocado showing.
1 **cup chopped green onions**	
3 **medium tomatoes, chopped**	6. Arrange chopped vegetables and Cheddar cheese in a pattern on top of the layers of dip. Serve with large tortilla chips.
2 **(3½ ounce) cans ripe olives**	
8 **ounces shredded sharp Cheddar cheese**	
Large tortilla chips	

"This dip is a tradition of Penn State Chicago alums at TV football parties."

John P. Fadden '70 Engl

Make your own tortilla chips by cutting soft tortillas in wedges and baking on a cookie sheet. The extra fat and salt of prepared ones is the only thing that is missing.

Eggplant Antipasto

PREPARATION TIME: *1 hour plus overnight chilling time*
YIELD: *36 ounces*

3 cups peeled and cubed eggplant	1. Sauté eggplant in oil until tender.
½ cup salad oil	2. Add the green pepper, mushrooms, garlic powder and onion. Cook slowly for 10 minutes.
⅓ cup chopped green pepper	
1 (4 ounce) can mushrooms	
½ teaspoon garlic powder	3. Add tomato paste, water, vinegar, olives, sugar, oregano, salt and pepper. Simmer for 30 minutes.
1 small onion, chopped	
1 (4 ounce) can tomato paste	4. Refrigerate overnight. Serve with crackers.
½ cup water	
2 teaspoons vinegar	
½ cup Spanish olives, chopped	
½ teaspoon sugar	
½ teaspoon oregano	
1 teaspoon salt	
1 teaspoon pepper	

Mary K. Walker
William R. Walker '40 C&F

Try broiling the eggplant to decrease fat and calories. You will elimi-nate 964 calories by not using the ½ cup oil.

28

Nittany Nachos

PREPARATION TIME: *1 hour*
YIELD: *8 servings*

¾ **pound ground beef**

1 **large onion, chopped**

1 **(4 ounce) can green chilies, chopped**

1 **tomato, chopped**

1 **jalapeño pepper, finely diced**

1 **cup salsa**

1 **(11 ounce) bag nacho chips**

1 **(16 ounce) can refried beans**

4 **ounces Monterey Jack cheese, shredded**

Sour cream

Avocado, mashed

1. Sauté ground beef and onion until meat is browned. Drain off grease.

2. Add chilies, tomato, and pepper. Stir mixture over low heat sautéing vegetables.

3. Add salsa and simmer over low heat.

4. Lightly grease a large oven proof quiche pan. Cover bottom of quiche dish with nachos. Spread refried beans over chips and top evenly with meat mixture.

5. Sprinkle cheese over meat mixture. Tuck nacho chips around the inside of the dish.

6. Bake uncovered at 400° for 25 – 30 minutes or until cheese has melted.

7. Serve with mounds of mashed avocado and dollops of sour cream.

Beth Orcutt Drude '80 Mktg, '83 MEd SplEd

Almost all refried beans contain lard, so watch labels carefully. Make your own, if necessary, to decrease fat. Browned ground beef can be cooked a day ahead, then stored in water in the refrigerator overnight. Skim fat before continuing recipe.

Roarin' Hot Mustard

PREPARATION TIME: *10 minutes plus 1 day*
YIELD: *2½ cups*

2 **cups dry mustard (8 ounces)**

2 **cups white vinegar**

2 **cups sugar**

2 **teaspoons salt**

4 **eggs, beaten**

1. Mix mustard and vinegar and let set overnight.

2. Next day add sugar, salt and eggs. Beat together until well mixed with electric mixer.

3. Pour into saucepan and bring to a boil. Boil for about 2 – 4 minutes, stirring occasionally. It will thicken. Store in a large container in refrigerator.

"This recipe was given to me by a Penn Stater a few years ago. Of course, we instantly remembered the mustard and pretzels we had consumed so often at the Train Station! This mustard is super with pretzels, cheese, chicken nuggets, etc. Better have a cool drink nearby."

Constance (Connie) Sullivan Yake '81 EKEd

Approximately 20,000 soft pretzels are sold each football game in Beaver Stadium.

Curried Sherry Pâté

PREPARATION TIME: *20 minutes*
YIELD: *15 – 20 servings*

6 ounces cream cheese

1 cup grated Cheddar cheese

½ teaspoon curry powder

½ teaspoon garlic powder

4 teaspoons sherry

¼ teaspoon salt

1 (9 ounce) jar chutney

½ cup chopped green onions, (tops too)

½ cup peanuts, chopped

½ cup bacon, crisp and chopped

1 hardboiled egg, chopped

½ cup toasted coconut

Assorted crackers

1. Blend first six ingredients thoroughly. Shape into a flat-topped round.

2. Score the cheese round into six sections.

3. Top each section with one of the next six ingredients.

4. Serve with assorted crackers.

Cheese round can be done day before. Assemble on day of serving.

Betty H. Dileanis
Col. (Ret.) Leonard P. Dileanis '48 MuEd

Shrimp Mousse

PREPARATION TIME: *30 minutes plus 2 days chilling time*
YIELD: *16 – 20 servings*

1 envelope unflavored gelatin

¼ cup cold water

1 (10¾ ounce) can tomato soup

8 ounces cream cheese

½ cup chopped green pepper

½ cup chopped onion

½ cup chopped celery

1 cup mayonnaise (Hellman's preferred)

2 (6½ ounce) cans small shrimp, drained

1. Dissolve gelatin in ¼ cup cold water; set aside.

2. Combine soup (undiluted) and cream cheese; warm over low heat until melted. Add gelatin mixture. Set aside and cool.

3. When gelatin mixture is cool add green pepper, onion, celery, mayonnaise, and shrimp; mix well. Place in mold and refrigerate for two days. Serve with plain crackers.

Marjorie Harris Burns '58 A&L

Green Pepper Spread

PREPARATION TIME: *15 minutes*
YIELD: *4 – 8 servings*

8 ounces cream cheese

½ cup butter

½ teaspoon salt

¼ teaspoon pepper

½ teaspoon mustard

¼ teaspoon paprika

¼ teaspoon Worcestershire sauce

3 teaspoons minced green pepper

1 – 2 tablespoons minced onion

1. In a medium bowl combine cream cheese, butter, salt, pepper, mustard, paprika, and Worcestershire sauce. Mix well.

2. Fold in green pepper and onion. Serve on party rye and pumpernickel.

During the Christmas season, use red and green minced pepper and garnish with slices of pepper on top.

Patricia Foley Bevers '70 GnAS

Sweet and Snappy Chutney Cheese

PREPARATION TIME: *30 minutes*
YIELD: *20 servings*

8 ounces cream cheese, softened	1. In large bowl of food processor with steel blade, place all ingredients, except crackers or apple wedges, process until well blended.
½ cup butter, softened	
¼ teaspoon dry English mustard	
¼ teaspoon freshly ground black pepper	2. Chill slightly.
	3. Mold into ball or loaf shape.
½ cup chutney	4. Wrap in waxed paper and refrigerate.
1 teaspoon curry powder	
2 teaspoons chutney for garnish	5. Before serving, spoon 2 teaspoons of chutney over the top.
Crackers or apple wedges	6. Serve with crackers or apple wedges.

Lois Bellmeyer Lynch '62 Journ

Apple wedges are a great change. At a party, allow guests to cut their own fresh apples by providing an apple slicer and a basket of a variety of apples. Non-fat plain yogurt or creamed soft tofu works well in place of cream cheese.

Chutney Cheese Ball

PREPARATION TIME: *5 minutes plus one hour chilling time*
YIELD: *10 – 12 servings*

8 ounces cream cheese, softened	1. Blend all the cheeses in a bowl with a wooden spoon until combined.
1 (5 ounce) jar Roquefort cheese spread	
1 (5 ounce) jar Cheddar cheese spread	2. Add chutney and combine well.
½ (9 ounce) jar chutney, chopped	3. Shape into a ball and cover with plastic wrap. Refrigerate for one hour. Roll in chopped walnuts. Serve with your favorite crackers.
½ cup chopped walnuts	

Carmelyn Baker
Benjamin J. Baker '73 CmpSc

Bleu Cheese Log

PREPARATION TIME: *30 minutes*
YIELD: *10 – 12 servings*

8 ounces cream cheese

3 ounces bleu cheese

2 tablespoons finely chopped celery

1 tablespoon finely chopped green onion

Mayonnaise to moisten

1½ cups chopped walnuts

1. Mix everything together except walnuts.

2. Shape into a log.

3. Roll in chopped walnuts and chill.

Mary Jane Dalton Roelofs '41 A&L

Nuts contain healthy protein, but are high in fat. Consider decreasing the amount — ½ cup walnuts maintains the flavor and crunch, decreases calories by 780!

Nittany Nibbles Cheese Squares

PREPARATION TIME: *20 minutes*
YIELD: *60 squares*

2 (5 ounce) jars sharp Cheddar cheese spread

1 cup butter

1 tablespoon Worcestershire sauce

Dash of Tabasco

2 loaves thin sandwich bread

1. Allow cheese and butter to come to room temperature. Combine and beat until light and fluffy with an electric mixer.

2. Add Worcestershire sauce and Tabasco.

3. Cut crusts from bread. Spread all slices with cheese and butter mixture (not too thick). Layer in stacks of three slices. Cut into four even squares and frost outsides with cheese and butter mixture.

4. Place on cookie sheet.

5. Bake at 350° for 15 minutes or until lightly browned.

This can be frozen for later use.

Carol Graham
John R. Graham '64, '65 MS AgE

Whole-grain breads contain more nutrients than white. Look for the word "whole" as the first ingredient on a bread label, whole wheat flour is the key.

Champion Cheese Balls

PREPARATION TIME: *30 minutes plus 20 minutes cooking time*
YIELD: *30 servings*

½ **cup butter, room temperature**

½ **pound American cheese, shredded at room temperature**

1 **cup flour**

½ **teaspoon salt**

½ **pound heat-and-serve pork sausage**

1. Combine butter and cheese in mixing bowl. Mix until smooth.

2. Add flour and salt. Mix well and form into a ball. Refrigerate dough until needed.

3. Cook sausage and drain. Cut sausage into bite-size portions.

4. Wrap sausage pieces with pieces of dough. Shape into balls.

5. Bake on an ungreased cookie sheet at 350° for 20 minutes or until lightly browned.

You can also use bulk sausage. Form it into walnut-size balls and then brown.

Marie Vergis Ferguson '69 EKEd

Beef Jerky

PREPARATION TIME: *1 day plus overnight baking*
YIELD: *25 – 35 pieces*

3 pounds lean beef, cut about 1 to 1¼ inches thick

1¼ cups inexpensive Burgundy wine

⅔ cup Worcestershire, soy, tempura or teriaki sauce (1 of these, or combine 2 or more)

2 teaspoons salt

½ teaspoon garlic salt, or 2 – 3 crushed garlic cloves

¼ teaspoon black pepper, herb pepper, or lemon pepper

1 large onion, sliced thinly

1. Place lean beef in freezer for 1 to 1½ hours; slice into thin (1/16 inch) strips (an electric knife is great for this; but any sharp knife will do)

2. Put sliced lean beef and all other ingredients into a 9 × 13-inch pan.

3. Marinate overnight at room temperature, covered with plastic wrap.

4. Place marinated sliced beef on wire racks on cookie sheets or over tin foil. (Pieces may touch, but not overlap.)

5. Bake in oven at lowest setting (200° or less) for 6 – 10 hours, or until it is the way you like.

6. Refrigerate beef jerky if you're not going to eat it immediately. Keeps 2 or 3 weeks at room temperature, or many weeks if refrigerated.

"Great finger food to pass out on the way to the game, or to hold everyone while the more elaborate spread is being set up. Also a wonderful snack for active times; hiking, camping, cross-country skiing, etc., because it can be carried in a pocket in a zip-lock bag."

Venison may be substituted for the beef.

Diana R. Dunn '70 PhD PhEd

Bahr None Meatballs

PREPARATION TIME: *15 minutes plus 20 minutes cooking time*
YIELD: *12 servings*

1 pound lean ground beef

1 small onion, chopped

¼ cup bread crumbs

1 egg, beaten

¼ cup snipped fresh basil

¼ cup fresh parsley

¼ cup fresh chives

1 small clove garlic, minced (optional)

Salt and pepper, to taste

1 cup red wine

1 cup ketchup

1. Mix the ground beef, onion, bread crumbs, egg, basil, parsley, chives, garlic, salt and pepper together.

2. Shape into small meatballs and fry.

3. Drain on paper towels.

4. Combine wine and ketchup together in saucepan. Bring to a boil.

5. Add meatballs, cover and simmer for 15 minutes or until sauce thickens slightly.

6. Serve in chafing dish with toothpicks on side to spear individual meatballs.

Davies Bahr

Broil meatballs instead of frying them. Place meatballs, or any meat, on a rack to allow fat to drip away.

Swedish Meat Ball Hors D'Oeuvres

PREPARATION TIME: *1 hour plus 2 – 4 days marinating time*
YIELD: *8 – 10 servings*

½ cup fine dry bread crumbs

½ cup warm cream

½ pound beef

¼ pound veal

¼ pound pork

½ cup milk

2 egg yolks, slightly beaten

2 tablespoons minced onion

2 teaspoons salt

⅓ teaspoon pepper

⅛ teaspoon allspice

Parsley flakes, optional

Parmesan cheese, optional

Burgundy wine

Consommé

1. Soak crumbs in cream; combine crumbs and meats; mix thoroughly and add milk.

2. Add egg yolks, onion, and seasonings; form into tiny balls.

3. Brown meatballs on all sides in butter or oil.

4. Cover with Burgundy and marinate 2 – 4 days.

5. Reheat in consommé to cover.

6. Serve in chafing dish with small amount of consommé.

Meatloaf mix may be used if it contains beef, veal and pork.

"We always made the meat balls on Tuesday evening and soaked them until Saturday."

Cornelia C. Ferguson
T. Reed Ferguson Jr. '36 AEd

Nittany Lion Wings

PREPARATION TIME: *4 hours 30 minutes*

YIELD: *30 – 35 pieces*

3 pounds chicken drummettes

2 (4½ ounce) bottles red hot sauce

½ cup butter or margarine

1. Cook drummettes on a rack on a cookie sheet at 425° for 1 hour. (Do not crowd on rack.)

2. Turn halfway through cooking time.

3. Melt butter or margarine and add hot sauce.

4. Pour over cooked drummettes and marinate at room temperature for 2 – 3 hours (turning occasionally).

5. Place on rack again and broil 5 minutes on a side (or until crispy).

Great hot or cold!

Eileen Bershok Marder '70 EKEd

At homecoming, the Diner sold 24,000 stickies in one weekend.

Jordan's Not-So-Hot

PREPARATION TIME: *50 minutes*
YIELD: *60 squares*

---

8 – 10 canned jalapeño peppers

1 pound Cheddar cheese, grated

6 eggs, well beaten

Grated onion, to taste

Paprika, to taste

1. Cut jalapeños in half and rinse them under cool water, removing all seeds and membranes. Drain well and chop finely.

2. Spread half of the grated cheese over the bottom of 7 × 11-inch pan.

3. Sprinkle the chopped jalapeños evenly over the cheese and top with the remaining cheese.

4. Pour the beaten eggs over everything.

5. Sprinkle top with grated onion and paprika.

6. Bake at 350° for 30 – 40 minutes or until the pie is set and slightly browned.

7. Cool for 5 – 10 minutes. Cut into bite-size squares for serving.

For a milder version, substitute peeled, chopped green chilies for the jalapeño peppers. Allow for plenty of cool, liquid refreshment!

Jonelle L. Jordan '87 Honorary Alumna

Cocktail Spinach Quiche

PREPARATION TIME: *1 hour 30 minutes*
YIELD: *60 squares*

10 **eggs**

½ **cup flour**

1 **teaspoon baking powder**

1 **teaspoon salt**

1 **(10 ounce) package frozen chopped spinach, thawed**

½ **cup margarine, melted**

2 **cups small curd cottage cheese**

½ **pound Cheddar cheese, grated**

½ **pound Monterey Jack cheese, grated**

Onion powder (optional)

1. Beat eggs in large bowl. Mix in flour, baking powder and salt.

2. Squeeze thawed spinach very well and add to egg mixture, along with melted margarine and the cheeses. Pour into a 9 × 13-inch pan.

3. Bake at 400° for 15 minutes. Reduce heat to 350° and bake an additional 35 – 40 minutes.

4. Let stand 5 minutes to set. Cut into 60 squares for hors d'oeuvres.

Janet Cmiel Nuhfer '73 MedT

New Mexican Egg Appetizer

PREPARATION TIME: *1 hour 15 minutes*
YIELD: *10 servings*

12 **eggs**

Chili powder to taste

3 **(7 ounce) cans green chili peppers, diced**

2 **pounds sharp Cheddar cheese, grated**

1. In large mixing bowl combine eggs and chili powder.

2. Drain juice from chili peppers into eggs.

3. In a greased 9 × 13-inch pan, spread half of the grated cheese.

4. Top cheese with half of the green chilies.

5. Repeat layers.

6. Beat eggs with fork and pour over the cheese and green chilies.

7. Bake at 350° for 1 hour. Slice into squares.

Two or three chopped jalapeño peppers may be used in addition to the green chilies for added "kick." This recipe freezes well and reheats well in oven or microwave.

Virginia (Ginny) Stumbaugh Krenzer '80 BLog

Hanky Panky

PREPARATION TIME: *30 minutes*
YIELD: *15 – 18 servings*

1 **pound ground beef**

1 **pound medium or hot pork sausage**

1 **pound Velveeta, cut up**

½ **teaspoon oregano**

½ **teaspoon garlic or onion salt**

2 **loaves cocktail rye bread or French baguettes**

1. In large skillet brown beef and sausage. Drain.

2. In medium saucepan combine meat mixture, cheese, oregano and garlic or onion salt. Cook and stir over medium heat until cheese is melted.

3. Spread mixture on slices of bread. Broil until lightly browned, watching closely.

Bread may be spread with mixture and frozen if desired.

Diana Ciclamino Short '78 MEd HlEd

Leah's Champion Appetizers

PREPARATION TIME: *20 minutes*
YIELD: *2 cups*

½ **cup chopped black olives**

½ **cup shredded Swiss cheese**

½ **cup mayonnaise**

½ **cup chopped onion**

½ **teaspoon salt**

Party rye or thin sliced bread

1. In medium bowl combine olives, Swiss cheese, mayonnaise, onion and salt.

2. Spread on one side of bread slices. Place slices on large cookie sheets.

3. Bake at 350° for 10 minutes.

Yvonne (Dolly) Fino Donovan '55 HEc

44

Parmesan Rounds

PREPARATION TIME: *8 minutes*
YIELD: *15 slices*

½ **cup mayonnaise**

½ **cup finely chopped onion**

½ **cup Parmesan cheese**

Party rye or pumpernickel bread

Paprika (optional)

1. In small bowl mix mayonnaise, onion and cheese together.

2. Spread generously on party rye or pumpernickel bread, covering to the edges.

3. Sprinkle with paprika if desired.

4. Broil until bubbly and lightly browned, about 3 minutes.

VARIATION: Add ½ can deviled ham or ½ cup chopped pepperoni.

Charmasielle L. Swope
James G. Swope Jr. '60 BA

Crabbies

PREPARATION TIME: *25 minutes plus 20 minutes freezing time*
YIELD: *48 servings*

½ **cup butter**

1 **(5 ounce) jar Olde English cheese spread**

1 **(6 ounce) can crab meat**

1 **teaspoon garlic powder**

Pepper, to taste

6 **English muffins, split**

1. Melt butter and cheese together.

2. Stir in crab meat, garlic powder and pepper.

3. Spread on split muffins.

4. Cut each muffin half into quarters.

5. Place on baking sheets and freeze for at least 20 minutes.

6. Bake at 450° for 2 – 3 minutes, then broil 2 – 3 more minutes or until bubbly and golden brown.

JoAnne Johnson Beach '77 IRE

English muffins are available in the whole wheat variety.

Hot Savory Pretzels

PREPARATION TIME: *10 minutes*
YIELD: *4 cups*

¼ **cup butter or margarine**	1. Microwave butter or margarine in large glass bowl on high, until melted.
2 **teaspoons dried parsley, crumbled**	2. Stir in parsley, tarragon, garlic powder and celery salt.
1 **teaspoon dried tarragon, crumbled**	3. Add pretzels and toss to coat.
¼ **teaspoon garlic powder**	4. Microwave on high for 3 minutes, stirring twice during cooking time. Serve immediately.
¼ **teaspoon celery salt**	
4 **cups small pretzels**	

Deborah Dean

Use whole grain pretzels, often with sesame seeds instead of salt, to increase fiber.

Cheese Biscuits

PREPARATION TIME: *30 minutes plus 10 minutes baking time*
YIELD: *8 – 10 servings*

1 **cup margarine**	1. Mix the margarine, flour and cheese together. Chill.
2 **cups flour**	2. Roll out to ¼ inch thick and cut with 1½ inch round cutter or a table glass.
8 **ounces grated New York extra sharp cheese**	3. Place on an ungreased cookie sheet and top each with half a pecan or walnut.
Pecan or walnut halves	4. Bake at 400° for 10 minutes.

Patricia Wright

Lady Lions Hot Hors D'Oeuvres

PREPARATION TIME: *15 minutes plus 15 minutes cooking time*
YIELD: *8 – 10 servings*

1 (2½ ounce) jar dried beef, snipped into small pieces

8 ounces cream cheese

2 tablespoons milk

2 tablespoons instant minced onion

⅛ teaspoon pepper

½ cup sour cream

¼ cup walnuts, chopped

1. Rinse dried beef well and dry on paper towels.

2. Blend all ingredients together, except walnuts. Place in a shallow baking dish.

3. Top with chopped walnuts.

4. Bake at 350° for 15 minutes. Serve with crispy crackers.

Barbara A. O'Reilly '72 MA Journ

Kick-Off Dates

PREPARATION TIME: *1 hour*
YIELD: *4 – 6 servings*

1 pound sliced bacon

1 pound pitted dates

1. Cut bacon strips in thirds.

2. Wrap each date with a piece of bacon.

3. Secure bacon to date with toothpick.

4. Place on a foil-lined jelly roll pan.

5. Bake at 350° until bacon is thoroughly cooked.

Serve hot, warm or room temperature.

Rita Apter Rolter '49 HEc

Diana's Nittany Snack

PREPARATION TIME: *40 minutes*
YIELD: *18 cups*

6 cups oatmeal

3 cups grapenuts cereal

2 cups coconut

2 cups nonfat dry milk

2 cups raisins

1 cup dried fruit, chopped

2 cups chopped walnuts

1½ cups sunflower seeds

1 cup chopped almonds

3 teaspoons cinnamon

1 teaspoon nutmeg

1½ cups oil

1½ cups honey

½ cup water

2 teaspoons vanilla

1. With a large spoon mix all dry ingredients together.

2. Heat oil, honey, and water together. Add vanilla and then mix with dry ingredients. Stir until all ingredients are moistened. Spread mixture on two or three cookie sheets with sides.

3. Bake at 350° for 10 minutes.

"Great as a dry snack or eat with milk for breakfast or on camping and backpacking trips."

Great to take into the game in a plastic bag.

Diana Lynn Neil
Larry W. Neil '77 2MngT

This healthy snack could be further enhanced by cutting the coconut to 1 cup and adding 1 teaspoon coconut extract and 1 teaspoon almond extract. Cut oil and honey in half to decrease calories and fat.

Final Yard Fruit Punch

PREPARATION TIME: *5 minutes*
YIELD: *1¼ gallons*

1 (6 ounce) can frozen lemonade

1 (8 ounce) can crushed pineapple

1 (10 ounce) package frozen strawberries

3 quarts ginger ale

1½ cups vodka

1. Mix lemonade, pineapple and strawberries in blender on high. Refrigerate until serving time.

2. Add ginger ale and vodka.

3. Serve over ice.

Joyce Koch Deem '70 SocW

Use unsweetened pineapple packed in water or its own juice. Frozen strawberries also are available without sugar. To keep the "fizz" without the calories, substitute club soda or seltzer water for the ginger ale.

Stately Slush

PREPARATION TIME: *15 minutes plus 24 hours freezing time*
YIELD: *5 quarts*

2 cups sugar

4 cups strong hot tea

12 ounces frozen lemonade

12 ounces frozen orange juice

10½ cups water

12 ounces whiskey

1. In a large 6-quart bowl dissolve sugar into hot tea.

2. Add remaining ingredients; stir throughly. Divide into plastic containers. Freeze for at least 24 hours.

3. Thaw slightly before serving.

"This is a great tailgate recipe, especially during hot weather. Do mark containers before putting in freezer."

Patricia Rutland Krone
Clair R. Krone '57, '61 MEd MuEd

Caged Lion

PREPARATION TIME: *10 minutes*
YIELD: *1 drink*

5 parts orange pineapple juice

1 part vodka

1 part rum

½ part grenadine

1. Mix all ingredients in a large container. Stir well.

2. Serve over ice in large iced tea glass.

Gerald (Jerry) T. Krivda '79 Math

Lion's Libation

PREPARATION TIME: *25 minutes*
YIELD: *8 cups*

1 quart apple cider or apple juice

1½ cinnamon sticks

1 teaspoon whole cloves

1 teaspoon whole allspice

Scant 3 ounces frozen orange juice concentrate

Scant 3 ounces lemonade concentrate

½ bottle (about 14 ounces) dry white wine

2 cups water

6 – 7 tablespoons brown sugar, to taste

Fruit slices for garnish

1. In large saucepan over high heat combine cider, cinnamon, cloves and allspice; bring to a boil.

2. Reduce heat to low; cover and simmer for 15 minutes.

3. Add frozen orange juice concentrate, lemonade concentrate, white wine, water and brown sugar to cider mixture.

4. Heat to boiling over high heat. Cool slightly and strain into punch bowl. Garnish with fruit slices.

Mary-Ellen Tietjen
James J. Tietjen '58 MS, '63 PhD FSc

Use a large "tea ball" or cheesecloth for cloves and allspice, so there's no need to strain after heating.

Sneaky Play

PREPARATION TIME: *15 minutes plus overnight freezing*
YIELD: *20 – 25 servings*

12 ounces frozen lemonade

12 ounces frozen orange juice

2 cups cranberry juice

2 cups powdered sugar

2 quarts 7-Up

1 fifth vodka

1. Mix all ingredients together.

2. Put into a large container and freeze overnight, stirring occasionally.

3. Remove from freezer and transfer to a punch bowl. Mixture will be slushy. Enjoy.

Jeanne Livingston Renton
William H. Renton '47 MngE

Consider the great blend of flavors, but with fewer sugar calories. So use unsweetened juices, decrease the sugar and substitute club soda or seltzer water for the 7-Up.

Irish Cream With Penn State Spirit

PREPARATION TIME: *10 minutes plus 48 hours chilling time*
YIELD: *20 ounces*

4 eggs

1 (14 ounce) can sweetened condensed milk

1 teaspoon coconut extract

1 teaspoon vanilla

2 tablespoons chocolate syrup

¾ cup whiskey

1. Combine all ingredients in a blender and mix well.

2. Pour into a bottle and refrigerate for at least 48 hours.

3. Shake before using.

4. Keep refrigerated.

"Tastes as good as Bailey's Irish Cream at about one quarter the cost."

M. Jane Lauster Miller '58 HEc

Boyd and Chuck's Festivity Punch

PREPARATION TIME: *20 minutes*
YIELD: *25 – 30 servings*

2 **(46 ounce) cans unsweetened pineapple juice**

1 **quart apple juice**

2½ **quarts cranberry juice**

1½ **quarts water**

1½ **cups firmly packed brown sugar**

1 **lemon, sliced thin**

8 **sticks cinnamon**

3½ **teaspoons whole cloves**

3 **berries of whole allspice**

1 **quart rum, optional**

1. Combine all ingredients in a large pot (stainless steel is best as aluminum reacts to the acid in the juice).

2. Cook until the flavor of the spices permeates the brew. Try not to boil.

3. Just before serving, strain and add rum if desired.

Charles Blauser

Zinger Punch

PREPARATION TIME: *30 minutes plus chilling time*
YIELD: *1 gallon*

6 **Red Zinger tea bags (Celestial Seasonings)**

2 **quarts water**

2 **quarts Tropicana Supreme orange juice**

Juice of 2 lemons

Juice of 2 limes

Juice of 2 navel oranges

½ **cup clover honey**

1. Boil or make sun tea with teabags and 2 quarts of water.

2. Add remaining ingredients.

3. Chill and serve.

Donald M. Schuler '75 GnAS

Strawberry Lemonade Punch

PREPARATION TIME: *15 minutes plus freezing time*
YIELD: *20 servings*

2 **(10 ounce) boxes frozen strawberries**

3 **(12 ounce) cans frozen lemonade**

¼ **cup fresh lemon juice**

6 **cups water**

1. Liquify strawberries in blender.

2. Add strawberries to lemonade concentrate.

3. Add lemon juice

4. Stir and freeze mixture.

5. Remove from freezer a few hours before serving.

6. Add water and stir slush.

7. Pour into punch bowl. Float an ice ring on top.

Fresh strawberries or lemon slices may be floated as garnish.

This punch became so popular with students and parents that we used it for many other social events in the college, so the students and faculty always referred to it as Human Development Punch.

R. Evelyn Replogle Saubel '35 HEc

The Behrend College owns a vineyard.

Extra Point Juice

PREPARATION TIME: *10 minutes plus chilling time*
YIELD: *3 gallons*

6 (.34 ounce) packs strawberry Koolade, (make up with sugar and water as if using four packs)

1 (46 ounce) can pineapple juice

1 (6 ounce) can frozen lemonade

2 (12 ounce) cans frozen orange juice

2 (46 ounce) cans red fruit drink

2 quarts ginger ale or 7-Up

1. Mix all ingredients together except ginger ale or 7-Up; chill.

2. Add the soda just before serving.

Betty Buss
C. Raymond Buss Jr. '51, '59 MEd PhEd

Mint Tea

PREPARATION TIME: *15 minutes*
YIELD: *1 gallon*

1 quart boiling water

2 family-size tea bags or 4 regular-size

1½ cups sugar

1 (12 ounce) can frozen orange juice (diluted)

1 (12 ounce) can frozen lemonade (diluted)

½ teaspoon peppermint flavor

1. Steep tea bags in boiling water for 10 minutes.

2. Remove tea bags and add sugar; stir until dissolved.

3. Add diluted orange juice and lemonade (dilute according to directions on the cans).

4. Add peppermint flavor.

5. Serve over ice.

Jan M. Bowman '69 SPA

Ideas for Entrée to Appetizer Conversions

The shrimp in Crevettes à la Lion on page 167 can easily be made into appetizers. Spoon a little of the mixture onto small seashells placed on a cookie sheet to bake. Adjust the baking time. Present one or two shells against a dramatic background of a bright green leaf on a small plate for a beautiful first course to start your next sit-down dinner.

If you like sautéed scallops enhanced by a favorite sherry sauce, place one large (or bite-sized) scallop with a little of the sauce in a small seashell. Offer the tiny shells on a large tray with cocktail forks. Grilled lobster pieces or bites of salmon are great presented that way, too. Or wrap a bite-sized piece of shellfish in a little square of thawed puff pastry (from the supermarket). Fold the squares diagonally in half and form triangles. Moisten the edges with water; press to seal with tines of a fork. Bake and serve right away or freeze them, unbaked, on baking sheets and then transfer to airtight containers. To serve, heat oven to 400 degrees, brush the tops of the triangles with a beaten egg, piece tops with a fork and bake on an ungreased baking sheet until lightly browned (15-20 minutes).

Soups/Sandwiches

Penn State Alumni Clubs entertain, too! They meet formally and informally, with simple refreshments or an entertaining menu. Some plan elaborate themes.

The Penn State Club of Greater Dayton sponsors a successful annual theme party — an ethnic soiree. The club invites undergraduate students. Ethnic food and games are the day's attraction and party-goers are encouraged to dress with a native flair. Past theme parties include a Mexican Fiesta, a German Augustfest (held in August!), a Japanese Sushi, an Italian Extravaganza and a Polish Luau (a kielbasa barbecue). Members of the club prepare all the food!

Every nation — including our own — seems to have special soups and sandwiches. The combination can be a most nutritious and satisfying meal as well as quick and easy, and most soups freeze well.

Use the recipes and ideas in this chapter to spark your imagination. Try the Happy Valley Cheese Soup, Hot and Sour Soup, or one of several Italian sandwiches. Note that the Muffulettas from New Orleans are simply an adaptation of an idea. If you bring back a food idea from one of your trips, you can usually reproduce it through trial and error. Or better yet, bring home a cookbook from the region you are visiting.

The soup and sandwich menu for parties is a pleasure for all age groups and can be developed in several ways. One idea is to have two pots of soup on the stove, an array of delicious sandwich fillings and your largest breadboard featuring a variety of bread and rolls — pumpernickel, rye, whole wheat, and multi-grain. Children especially enjoy making their own sandwiches. In fact, for a children's party, try using colorful paper "nut cups" for fillings (peanut butter, jelly, egg salad, and ham spread for example). Each child helps himself to his own delight — little spreaders, plates, and small party-size loaves of bread.

If your soup tureen is currently holding a floral arrangement on your mantle, other great containers for soup are punch bowls, earthenware crocks, hollowed-out pumpkins, good-looking range-to-table ware, and stock pots presented in a casual setting. If your stock pot is aged from years of loving use, tie a colorful scarf around the pot to dress it up!

It's easy to garnish soups. Cube a few pieces of bread and toss into a frying pan with a little butter. Or simply bake the cubes in the oven. Snip the tops from your pots of herbs or the parsley in your refrigerator. Use a little grated cheese or a dollop of sour cream. A pretty flower placed on the plate beside the soup bowl is a nice garnish, and what a special one at that.

Cream of Pimento Soup

PREPARATION TIME: *30 minutes*
YIELD: *10 servings*

2 tablespoons butter

3 tablespoons flour

½ teaspoon salt

½ teaspoon grated onion

3 cups milk

4 cups chicken stock (fresh stock or stock made by dissolving 5 bouillon cubes in 4 cups boiling water)

½ cup pimentos

1. Melt butter; add flour, salt and onion. Blend well.

2. Add milk, stock and pimentos that have been put through sieve.

3. Cook 20 – 30 minutes; stir constantly until mixture thickens.

Corinne Joy Strasmyer
Robert H. Strasmyer '39 Arch

Mushroom-Wild Rice Soup

PREPARATION TIME: *1 hour*
YIELD: *8 – 10 servings*

1 (6 ounce) package long grain and wild rice mixture

⅓ cup butter or margarine

1 medium onion, finely chopped

½ pound fresh mushrooms, sliced

½ cup thinly sliced celery

½ cup flour

6 cups chicken broth

½ teaspoon curry powder

½ teaspoon dry mustard

¼ teaspoon white pepper

2 cups half and half

⅔ cup dry sherry

1. Prepare rice according to package directions.

2. In large saucepan, melt butter or margarine over medium heat; add onion, sauté about 5 minutes until golden.

3. Add mushrooms and celery. Cook while stirring for about 3 minutes.

4. Mix in flour. Gradually add broth, stir constantly until thickened, about 5 – 8 minutes.

5. Stir in rice and seasonings. Reduce heat to low.

6. Stir in half and half and sherry.

7. Stir occasionally while heating, but do not boil.

Best if made in advance so flavors can blend. Reheat gently.

George R. Bundy '65 ME

Low-sodium broth and canned evaporated skim milk are healthy substitutes in this recipe.

Hot and Sour Soup

PREPARATION TIME: *50 minutes*
YIELD: *4 – 6 servings*

4 **cups chicken stock**	1. Bring chicken stock to slow boil.
6 **ounces chicken or pork in julienne strips**	2. Add meat, tofu, and mushrooms. Cook 3 – 5 minutes; stirring occasionally.
½ **cup tofu**	
6 **cloud-ear mushrooms**	3. Combine soy sauce, sugar, salt, and cornstarch mixture.
1 **tablespoon soy sauce**	4. Add to soup, stirring until soup returns to a boil.
¼ **teaspoon sugar**	
¾ **teaspoon salt**	5. Stir soup slowly pouring in egg. Remove from heat.
2 **tablespoons cornstarch mixed with 3 tablespoons water**	6. Combine vinegar and pepper in a 1½-quart bowl.
1 **egg, lightly beaten**	
3 **tablespoons Chinese red vinegar**	7. Add soup and onions. Stir and serve immediately.
¼ **teaspoon white pepper**	
2 **green onions, thinly sliced including tops**	

James A. Haworth

Tofu, soy cheese, is a wonderful low-cholesterol, low-calorie protein. It picks up the flavor of the sauce/foods you put with it.

Happy Valley Cheese Soup

PREPARATION TIME: *20 minutes*

YIELD: *4 servings*

1 **medium onion, chopped**

1 **green pepper, chopped**

½ **cup butter**

2 **(16 ounce) cans kidney beans, drained**

8 **ounces Velveeta cheese, cut up**

1 **cup water**

1. Sauté onion and pepper in butter until soft, but not brown.

2. Add rest of ingredients and heat until cheese is melted.

3. Do not boil and do not add more water.

4. Serve with hard rolls and a tossed salad.

Marguerite (Peggy) Scheaffer Washabaugh '40 A&L

Broccoli Cheese Soup

PREPARATION TIME: *30 minutes*
YIELD: *5 cups*

2 tablespoons finely chopped onions

2 tablespoons butter

3 tablespoons flour

½ teaspoon salt

⅛ teaspoon pepper

2 cups milk

1 cup shredded American cheese

2 chicken bouillon cubes

1½ cups water

1 bay leaf

1 (10 ounce) package frozen chopped broccoli

1. In large saucepan, cook onions in butter until tender.

2. Stir in flour, salt, and pepper until well blended.

3. Add milk all at once. Cook until thickened, stirring constantly.

4. Add cheese and stir until melted. Remove from heat.

5. In medium saucepan dissolve bouillon cubes in water. Add bay leaf and bring to a boil.

6. Add broccoli and cook according to package directions; do not drain.

7. Add broccoli and cooking liquid to cheese mixture; stir until well blended.

8. Remove bay leaf and serve.

Moderately easy. Can freeze. Can do ahead. Can double easily.

Carol Hollinger Moyer '76 EKEd

Canned evaporated skim milk would decrease fat and calories.

Nittany Lion's Roarin' Minestrone

PREPARATION TIME: *1 hour 15 minutes*
YIELD: *6 – 8 servings*

2 tablespoons olive oil

1½ cups coarsely chopped onion

2 cloves garlic, minced

1 cup thinly sliced carrots

1 cup thinly sliced celery

1 cup chopped green pepper

1 quart unpeeled zucchini, cut in small cubes

2 cups green beans, cut into 1-inch pieces

1 (35 ounce) can Italian plum tomatoes, undrained

2 cups chicken broth or water

2 teaspoons basil leaves

½ teaspoon oregano leaves

Salt and pepper, to taste

½ cup uncooked elbow macaroni

1 (20 ounce) can chick-peas, drained

1 (20 ounce) can red kidney beans, drained

3 cups finely sliced cabbage

Chopped fresh parsley

1. In a pot or casserole with a capacity of at least 5 quarts, heat the oil.

2. Add onion, garlic, carrots, celery, and green pepper and sauté until the onion is tender.

3. Add the zucchini, green beans, tomatoes, broth, basil, oregano, salt, and pepper and mix gently. Cover and simmer slowly for 40 minutes. Stir occasionally.

4. Add macaroni, chick-peas, kidney beans, and cabbage. Cover and simmer about 15 minutes longer, or until the macaroni and cabbage are tender. Stir once or twice. (The soup will be thick, almost a stew. If you like a thinner soup, add more broth or water.)

5. Garnish lavishly with parsley before serving.

"This is a low-fat, high-fiber recipe! A thick and hearty soup that is a veritable cornucopia of vegetables."

Louise Keefer Fisher '63 A&L

Whole wheat pasta is a higher fiber alternative to white.

Ham-Broccoli Chowder

PREPARATION TIME: *5 – 7 hours*
YIELD: *4 – 6 servings*

¼ cup flour

1 (5 ounce) can evaporated milk

2 cups water

2 cups cubed baked ham

1 (10 ounce) package frozen broccoli spears, cut into pieces

¼ cup minced onion

½ pound grated Swiss cheese

1 cup light cream

1. Mix flour, milk and water in slow cooker (crockpot).

2. Add ham, broccoli, onion and cheese.

3. Cook on low 5 – 7 hours.

4. Before serving add cream and heat through.

Susan Johannesmeyer Grand '76 HPE

Canned evaporated "skim" milk is a good substitute. You could use another can for the light cream also, to save fat and calories.

Sam Gallu's Lima Bean Soup

PREPARATION TIME: *4 hours plus overnight soaking of beans*
YIELD: *12 – 16 servings*

2 **pounds small dried lima beans, sorted and rinsed**

4 **carrots, scraped and chopped**

4 **celery stalks, sliced**

1 **large onion, chopped**

2 **large garlic cloves, minced**

2 **bay leaves**

1 **large smoked ham hock**

3 **smoked pork chops**

1 **tablespoon salt**

Freshly ground black pepper, to taste

2 **pounds smoked sausage, cut into 2" lengths**

4 **pounds smoked spareribs, cut into 3" pieces, ribs separated**

2 **tablespoons Worcestershire sauce**

1. Soak the lima beans overnight in cold water to cover.

2. Drain and put the beans in a heavy 10-quart pot with the carrots, celery, onion, garlic, bay leaves, ham hock, pork chops, salt, pepper, and enough water to cover. Slowly bring to a boil. Immediately lower the heat and simmer, partially covered, for 1 hour and 30 minutes.

3. Add the sausage, ribs, and Worcestershire sauce. Mix well and cook for 1 hour and 30 minutes to 2 hours, or until the beans are tender and the meat is just about falling from the bones. Taste for seasoning.

Samuel G. Gallu '40 A&L

Fiesta Bowl Albondigas

PREPARATION TIME: *2 hours*
YIELD: *14 – 18 servings*

STOCK

5 (10¾ ounce) cans consommé or beef bouillon

5 cans water

2 (16 ounce) cans stewed tomatoes

1 soup can tomato juice

¼ small head cabbage, thinly sliced

1 cup celery leaves and chopped celery

2 cups any leftover mixed vegetables (carrots, peppers, peas, beans, etc.)

1 bay leaf

2 teaspoons salsa jalapeño (more if you want a hotter taste)

1 teaspoon freshly ground pepper

¼ cup red wine (your choice)

1. In an 8-quart kettle bring the first 8 ingredients to a boil and let simmer while you form the meatballs. Bring to a second boil and add meatballs a few at a time, keeping the liquid at a boil. When all meatballs have been added, skim any foam from top.

2. Stir in salsa jalapeño, pepper and wine.

3. Simmer for at least 30 minutes.

MEATBALLS

2 pounds ground beef

1½ teaspoons salt

1½ teaspoons chili powder

1 onion, grated

2 tablespoons parsley flakes

¼ teaspoon minced garlic

1 cup soft bread crumbs

2 eggs, slightly beaten

½ cup slivered almonds or piñon nuts

1. In a medium bowl blend together all ingredients with fork or hands and roll into walnut size meatballs. Makes about 3 dozen.

Nancy Fry Doutt '51

Keep small amounts of leftover vegetables in the freezer. Add to them as you can for a lovely combination in recipes like this.

Tailgate Stew

PREPARATION TIME: *45 minutes plus 5 hours cooking time*
YIELD: *6 – 8 servings*

2 pounds beef, cut in bite-size pieces

4 carrots, chopped

4 potatoes, chopped

2 onions, chopped

2 cloves garlic, chopped

1 teaspoon parsley

⅛ teaspoon marjoram

⅛ teaspoon oregano

⅛ teaspoon rosemary

⅛ teaspoon basil

Salt and pepper, to taste

1 (4 ounce) can mushrooms

2 (10½ ounce) cans tomato soup

½ cup water

1. Combine and mix all ingredients together.

2. Place in a Dutch oven and bake at 275° for 5 hours.

3. Serve over rice or plain.

Can also cook in a crockpot for 5 hours.

Jackie L. Singel
Honorable Mark S. Singel '74 Engl

Artichoke Lamb Stew

PREPARATION TIME: *20 minutes plus 2 hours cooking*
YIELD: *6 – 8 servings*

3 – 4 pounds lamb, cubed	1. Season meat with salt and pepper.
Salt and pepper, to taste	2. Heat oil in Dutch oven, add meat, turning each piece over, but *do not* brown.
¼ cup olive oil	
2 large onions, chopped	3. Spread onions over meat.
½ cup dry white wine	4. Stir together the wine, tomato paste, vinegar, honey, garlic, thyme, currants and orange peel. Pour over onions.
1 (16 ounce) can tomato paste	
2 tablespoons vinegar	
1 tablespoon honey	5. Cover and cook over very low heat for 2 hours. *Do not* stir.
2 garlic cloves, crushed	
1½ teaspoons crumbled thyme	6. Add artichokes, submerging them in the liquid.
2 tablespoons currants	
Orange peel	7. Cover again and simmer 4 – 5 minutes.
2 (9 ounce) packages frozen artichokes, thawed	8. Just before serving add parsley and very gently stir stew to blend.
Freshly chopped parsley	

Janice Krauss Shapiro '74 IFS

Hunter's Stew

PREPARATION TIME: *3 hours*

YIELD: *4 – 6 servings*

4 pounds wild game meat (grouse, pheasant, woodcock, duck, quail, crow, moose, venison, elk, bobcat, rabbit, coyote, bear, squirrel, etc.)

6 carrots

6 potatoes

3 onions

1 cup red wine

½ cup red wine vinegar

1 clove garlic, crushed

2 bay leaves

1 teaspoon salt

½ teaspoon sherry pepper sauce or hot pepper sauce

3 – 4 beef bouillon cubes

1. Place meat in a covered pot with 3 – 4 cups of water. Boil for 45 minutes to an hour until meat is tender. Remove meat from bones, dice and return meat to pot.

2. Cut vegetables into bite-size pieces; add to meat. Add wine, vinegar, garlic, seasonings and bouillon cubes; simmer for 1 – 2 hours.

3. Serve immediately or cool and refrigerate to serve later.

"Great with wild rice and wine or beer. A game supper delight. You can also add a shot of brandy or cognac 5 minutes before removing from heat."

Alvin L. Barth Jr. '58 Metal

Although wild game is generally leaner than other meats, you might chill the cooked mixture overnight and skim off extra fat. Eliminating the salt and using low-sodium bouillon cubes is another idea for making this stew even more healthy.

Tailgate Chili

PREPARATION TIME: *3 hours*

YIELD: *6 – 10 servings*

½ – 1 pound ground beef

2 medium white onions, diced

2 celery stalks, diced

1 large green pepper, diced

2 (14 ounce) cans kidney beans

1 tablespoon salt

2 (14 ounce) cans whole tomatoes, diced or 8 fresh tomatoes diced

1 tablespoon chili powder

1 tablespoon herb seasoning

1 teaspoon ground pepper

1 cup water

1. Brown ground beef in 4-quart pan. Drain grease.

2. Add onion, celery, peppers, kidney beans, tomatoes, spices and water. Simmer over low heat for 2 – 2½ hours, stirring frequently.

Spice amounts can be increased/decreased according to taste.

Robert P. Rehkopf '50 ZE

Low-sodium versions of herb seasonings are available from many companies. Choose blends that fit your taste and cooking style.

Fireball Chili

PREPARATION TIME: *2 hour 30 minutes*
YIELD: *5 – 7 servings*

1 **pound ground beef**

1½ **teaspoons garlic powder**

1 **onion, chopped**

1 **(2 pound 8 ounce) can kidney beans**

1 **(15 ounce) can tomato sauce**

1 **(10¾ ounce) can tomato soup**

1 **tablespoon chili powder**

1 **teaspoon black pepper**

½ **teaspoon dried crushed red pepper**

1 **(15 ounce) can stewed tomatoes**

1. Brown beef with garlic and onion. Drain.

2. Add remaining ingredients. Cook uncovered for two hours over very low heat. Chili should just barely simmer. Serve with crackers, corn chips, and Cheddar cheese.

"Great for tailgates or for watching games at home. Also good for a hearty winter meal."

Carolyn L. Hughey '82 Anthy

Prepare ground beef ahead of time, cover with water and refrigerate. Skim fat from top (before continuing recipe) to decrease fat and calories.

Vegetarian Chili

PREPARATION TIME: *30 minutes plus 8 hours cooking time*
YIELD: *8 servings*

½ bunch celery and leaves, chopped coarsely

2 green peppers, cleaned and chopped coarsely

3 cloves garlic, minced (optional)

1 large onion, chopped

2 (16 ounce) cans whole tomatoes (do not drain)

2 pounds canned red beans or kidney beans, drained

½ cup raisins

1 tablespoon chili powder (or to taste)

1 tablespoon snipped parsley

1½ teaspoons dried basil, crushed

1½ teaspoons dried oregano, crushed

1 teaspoon ground cumin

1 teaspoon ground allspice

¼ teaspoon pepper

¼ teaspoon bottled hot pepper sauce

2 bay leaves

1 pound dry beans (any red/ kidney dried beans)

¾ cup dry roasted cashew nuts

8 ounces mozzarella cheese, grated

1. Place all ingredients, except dried beans, nuts and mozzarella cheese, in crockpot and cook all day.

2. Place dry beans in enough water to cover generously. Bring to a boil and then simmer for 2 – 3 hours until soft and well thickened.

3. Add cooked beans and roasted nuts to crockpot ingredients. Heat well for 30 minutes.

4. Remove bay leaves and serve.

5. Sprinkle top of each serving with grated mozzarella cheese.

Amy Shetter Shuman '69 FSHA
John D. Shuman '69 FSHA

Cajun Chicken Sandwich

PREPARATION TIME: *25 minutes*
YIELD: *6 sandwiches*

3 whole chicken breasts, halved and boned

Cajun spice, available at specialty stores

6 onion rolls

6 teaspoons mayonnaise

6 leaves lettuce

1 Spanish onion, sliced thin

2 tomatoes, sliced thin

1. Remove fat from chicken breasts and pound until thin. Sprinkle cajun spice on both sides of chicken.

2. In a large skillet over medium-low heat, cook chicken on both sides until chicken is white.

3. Slice onion rolls in half. Place one teaspoon mayonnaise on each roll, top with lettuce, onion, and tomato slices.

4. Place a piece of chicken on each roll and enjoy.

Chicken can be cooked ahead of time for tailgating; could also be grilled at tailgate.

Elaine F. Given

National Champion Hamwich

PREPARATION TIME: *30 minutes*
YIELD: *12 large sandwiches*

1 pound chipped ham

½ pound grated Cheddar cheese

3 hard-cooked eggs, chopped

¾ (12 ounce) bottle chili sauce

3 heaping tablespoons salad dressing, preferably mayonnaise

3 tablespoons chopped onions (or less)

½ cup chopped olives

12 sandwich rolls

1. Mix all ingredients together. Put into rolls and wrap in aluminum foil.

2. Bake at 350° for 20 minutes.

Grace Miller Stover '50 Ed
Ward M. Stover '51 AgEd, '81 MEd ExtEd

Nittany Victory Sandwiches

PREPARATION TIME: *30 minutes*
YIELD: *6 – 8 servings*

½ **pound ground beef**

1 **pound mild Italian sausage**

1 **small green pepper, chopped**

¾ **cup chopped onion**

¼ **cup sliced mushrooms**

1 **(8 ounce) can tomato sauce**

1 **(8 ounce) can tomato paste**

¼ **cup water**

¼ **cup grated Parmesan cheese**

⅛ **teaspoon oregano**

1 **loaf Vienna bread**

6 **ounces mozzarella cheese, sliced**

1. Combine ground beef and sausage in skillet and brown over medium heat; drain.

2. Add green pepper, onion and mushrooms; cook 3 – 5 minutes.

3. Add tomato sauce, paste, water, Parmesan, and oregano. Mix well and cook over medium heat for 10 minutes; stirring constantly.

4. Cut (lengthwise) one slice from top of Vienna bread; set aside. Remove center of bread, forming a shell.

5. Place half of the mozzarella cheese on bottom of the shell. Fill with hot meat mixture. Cover with remaining cheese slices and cover with slice of bread. Wrap in aluminum foil.

6. Bake at 400° for 6 – 8 minutes. Remove foil and slice into sandwiches.

Kathy DeVivo Pesta '79 EKEd

Muffulettas

PREPARATION TIME: *2 – 3 hours*
YIELD: *15 – 20*

OLIVE SALAD

1 (13 ounce) jar green salad olives

1 carrot, diced

1 celery stalk, diced

1 large onion, diced

1 teaspoon oregano

½ teaspoon sweet basil

1 teaspoon garlic powder

2 tablespoons parsley flakes

¾ cup olive oil

1. Drain brine from olives and refill jar with water. Let stand at least 15 minutes. Drain again and let stand 15 minutes and drain. Taste olives. If you think they are still too salty, repeat the water bath.

2. Drain olives well and dice.

3. Mix the olives, carrot, celery, onion, seasonings and olive oil together.

4. Let stand about two hours to marinate. Taste. Additional seasonings can be added to suit your taste.

SANDWICH

1½ dozen hard Italian rolls

1 pound Capicola ham, sliced

1 pound Genoa salami, sliced

1 pound provolone cheese, sliced

1. Place at least one slice ham, salami, and cheese on each roll.

2. To make room for the olive salad, hollow out one side of sliced roll. Place a large tablespoon of salad in the hollow.

3. Heat in microwave or regular oven until thoroughly heated.

Josephine Eyer

BBQ-Better Be Quick

PREPARATION TIME: *1 hour 15 minutes*

YIELD: *6 – 8 servings*

1 cup ketchup

¼ – ½ cup chopped onions

½ cup water

2 tablespoons brown sugar

½ teaspoon salt

Dash of pepper

2 tablespoons vinegar

3 tablespoons Worcestershire sauce

½ tablespoon mustard

½ cup chopped celery

1½ – 2 pounds chipped ham (pork or beef can be substituted)

Onion rolls

1. In a 2-quart baking dish combine the first ten ingredients well. Then add meat.

2. Bake covered, at 350° for 1 hour.

3. Serve on onion rolls.

"Great at any PSU tailgate party."

Lorrie L. Miller

Try leftover skinned chicken or turkey, for a leaner version. The great flavor is in the sauce, so no one will mind your healthy attitude.

Sausage and Mushroom Barbecue

PREPARATION TIME: *2 hours*
YIELD: *25 – 30 sandwiches*

3 pounds Italian sausage, casing removed

1 (6 ounce) can tomato sauce

1 small onion, chopped

1 tablespoon sugar

½ teaspoon salt

½ teaspoon oregano

16 ounces mushrooms, sliced

1 (12 ounce) can tomato paste

1 medium green pepper, chopped

1 clove garlic, minced

1½ cups water

1. Cook sausage in large pot until well done. Break into small chunks while cooking. After sausage is cooked, drain off all grease.

2. Place all other ingredients in separate sauce pot, stir, cover, and simmer for 1 hour.

3. If sauce becomes too thick, add water. (If canned mushrooms are used, pour in liquid from can.)

4. After sauce has simmered, pour over sausage. Mix well, cover, and simmer for another 30 minutes.

5. Serve hot on hard rolls.

"This recipe is great for large gatherings, such as graduation parties, picnics and birthday parties. Also great for tailgate parties."

Theresa M. Milore '86 AdmJ

Lower Allen Barbecue

PREPARATION TIME: *50 minutes*

YIELD: *6 servings*

1 pound ground beef	1. In a large skillet sauté beef and onion; drain fat.
1 large onion	
½ cup ketchup	2. Add remaining ingredients and simmer 40 minutes. Serve in buns.
½ cup chili sauce	
1 teaspoon prepared mustard	
1 tablespoon Worcestershire sauce	
Salt, to taste	
Pepper, to taste	

Jeannine Bell LeVan '52 Ed

80

Happy Valley Burgers

PREPARATION TIME: *30 minutes plus 10 minutes cooking*
YIELD: *8 – 10 burgers*

6 cherry tomatoes, diced

6 fresh mushrooms, diced

½ green pepper, diced

1 small onion, diced

2 pounds lean ground beef

8 – 10 slices bacon

1. Mix the diced tomatoes, mushrooms, pepper and onion with the ground beef.

2. Form into 8 – 10 hamburger patties.

3. Heat the bacon until it separates easily.

4. Wrap a strip of bacon around the edge of each burger and secure with a toothpick.

5. Grill. (Have water handy to quell grease flare-ups.)

6. Remove toothpicks and serve.

Can do ahead up until cooking.

Jane Clarke Wettstone '67 EKEd
Jerry R. Wettstone '62 PhEd, '63 MEd ReEd

Try lean ground turkey in place of beef. If you grind your own or ask the butcher to do so, you avoid the "up to 29% fat" allowed in pre-packaged ground turkey.

Penn State's bakery makes 250,000 dozen hamburger rolls a year.

Penn State Blue Burgers

PREPARATION TIME: *30 minutes*
YIELD: *4 burgers*

½ cup chopped onions

3 tablespoons butter

2 tablespoons flour

¼ teaspoon salt

1 cup milk

½ cup crumbled bleu cheese

1 pound ground beef

Buttered French bread

1. Sauté onions in butter; stir in flour and salt.

2. Add milk and bring to a boil. Remove from heat and stir in cheese. Stir until melted.

3. Shape ground beef into 4 patties and broil.

4. Serve patties on buttered French bread slices. Top with sauce.

Antoinette (Tonie) Leisey Allsopp '82 GnAS

Use skim milk to save 90 calories. Also, try rubbing a garlic clove or two over the cut French bread and toast. This eliminates the need for buttering.

Pizza Bread

PREPARATION TIME: *15 – 20 minutes*
YIELD: *12 – 15 slices*

1 loaf frozen bread dough, thawed

⅔ cup margarine

½ teaspoon oregano

1 teaspoon parsley

¼ teaspoon seasoned salt

2 cups grated provolone cheese

1 cup sliced pepperoni

1. Roll dough out into a rectangle (approximately 10 × 13-inch) on a floured board.

2. In saucepan, combine margarine, oregano, parsley, and seasoned salt. Brush mixture on bread (easier to spoon on; then spread evenly). Reserve some mixture for later use.

3. Cover with cheese and top with pepperoni.

4. Roll the bread lengthwise and pinch together at the seam. Place bread, seam down, on a greased cookie sheet or pizza pan. Bring ends together to form a ring. Brush outside of loaf with reserved seasoning mix.

5. Bake at 350° for 30 – 40 minutes or until golden brown. Just before finished baking sprinkle with additional cheese.

Bringing the ends together is optional, mainly for space-saving. The roll can be left as a loaf. For freezing cook only about 20 minutes; will take approximately 20 minutes to heat and finish cooking. Reheating can be done in microwave or on a grill. Best served hot, but good cold.

VARIATION: Substitute Corned beef, sauerkraut and Swiss cheese. Sprinkle top with caraway seeds for a Reuben loaf.

Kevin E. Still '83 Commu

Pane Italiano

PREPARATION TIME: *45 minutes*
YIELD: *4 large servings*

1	**large loaf Italian bread**
	Olive oil
2	**cups canned Italian plum tomatoes, drained**
½	**cup tomato sauce**
½	**teaspoon basil**
½	**teaspoon oregano**
¾	**teaspoon salt**
¼	**teaspoon pepper**
1	**small clove garlic, minced**
4	**ounces pepperoni, sliced**
4	**ounces Italian salami, diced**
4	**ounces mozzarella cheese, grated**
¼	**cup grated Romano cheese**

1. Cut a ½-inch slice off top of bread. Hollow out inside of loaf, leaving a ½-inch shell.

2. Brush inside and outside of loaf lightly with olive oil. Place on baking sheet and heat at 400° for 5 minutes, until inside is dry but not browned.

3. In a medium saucepan combine tomatoes, sauce, basil, oregano, salt, pepper, garlic, pepperoni, and salami. Heat to bubbling then lower heat and simmer 10 minutes.

4. Remove from heat and stir in mozzarella cheese.

5. Spoon mixture into hollowed out loaf and top with grated Romano cheese.

6. Bake at 400° for 10 – 15 minutes, until loaf is golden brown.

7. Cut into thick slices and serve hot.

"In 1972, I was enrolled in Nutrition 119. Since this particular course had a kitchen lab, we were constantly trying new recipes. On the last day of class/lab, we were to bring a recipe that we would make for the group. I found the Pane Italiano recipe in a magazine. My cooking partner and I made it for the class and it was a great success. Hence, the recipe had its beginnings in the hallowed halls of Penn State."

Lynda Johnson Sheffer '73 IFS

Party Boli

PREPARATION TIME: *2 hours 30 minutes*
YIELD: *3 – 4 servings*

1 loaf frozen bread dough	1. Thaw bread dough. Let rise, then punch down and let rise again.
Mustard (Dijon or regular)	
¼ pound sliced American cheese	2. Roll dough out into a 12 × 8-inch rectangle.
¼ pound sliced provolone cheese	3. Spread mustard on dough and layer meat and cheese on half of the bread dough.
¼ pound sliced ham	
¼ pound sliced Genoa salami	
Garlic powder	4. Sprinkle with garlic powder and oregano.
Oregano	5. Fold sides of dough over meat and cheese and roll to close. Pinch seams to close completely.
Olive oil	
"Jimbo" sauce	

6. Brush dough with olive oil and sprinkle more oregano on top.

7. Place on large cookie sheet and bake at 375° for 30 minutes.

8. Serve with "Jimbo" tomato sauce (for dipping).

"JIMBO" TOMATO SAUCE

1 (28 ounce) can crushed tomatoes

1 (6 ounce) can tomato paste

1 cup water

1 medium onion, chopped

2 cloves garlic, crushed

Pinch basil

1 small bay leaf

1 sliver green pepper, chopped

Salt and pepper, to taste

1. Combine all ingredients in large pot and simmer for 1 hour 30 minutes.

Patti Creghan-Ciuffetelli '79 2Rtl, '82 Bus

Pizza By The Football Yard

PREPARATION TIME: *20 minutes*
YIELD: *4 – 6 servings*

1 loaf French bread

1 tablespoon olive oil

2 cups pizza sauce

12 ounces mozarella cheese, shredded

¼ cup Parmesan cheese

Toppings

PIZZA SAUCE

2 tablespoons olive oil

1 large clove garlic

½ cup chopped onion

15 ounces tomato sauce

1½ teaspoons basil

1 teaspoon oregano

1. Slice the bread lengthwise and spread the cut sides with a light touch of olive oil.

2. Broil, cut side up, 3 – 4 inches from heat for 3 – 4 minutes or until golden.

3. Spread bread with pizza sauce, then top with cheeses.

4. Add your favorite pizza toppings. Broil for 1 minute or until cheese melts.

1. Sauté garlic and onion in olive oil until limp.

2. Add tomato sauce, basil, and oregano and simmer for fifteen minutes, uncovered.

"This recipe is a great imitation of the popular French bread pizzas."

Sandra Garo Haffner '78 GnAS

Approximately 32,000 hot dogs are sold each football game in Beaver Stadium.

86

Entertaining with International Flavor

Menus featuring ethnic foods are imaginative and yet are easy to plan. Clubs are an ideal vehicle for international entertaining because large groups will quickly become more involved in games, dancing, music, singing, and distinctive traditions (such as breaking open the Mexican piñata). Decorating for an international theme is easily researched: Japanese lanterns; beer steins and German flags; and masses of colorful flowers for a Polynesian party.

In personal entertaining as well, an international flavor is easy to develop as a theme. Begin with the invitations and carry out the idea with a musical and visual background (records and paintings can be borrowed from most local libraries). Tabletop accessories can be your travel souvenirs . . . Swiss bells, Indonesian batiks, or Fijian tapa cloth mats. Whatever you use will encourage wonderful conversations of actual journeys or sojourns wistfully imagined.

Cookbooks abound with international recipes, and often your own files reveal treasured ideas from your family backgrounds.

Salads/Vegetables/Side Dishes

Today, Penn State students enjoy a choice in the dining halls that many of us wish we could have had: the ever-popular salad bar! Stories of many a contest among friends to build the biggest and best salads abound! So, young Penn Staters are gaining experience and enthusiasm in preparing salads that are the most imaginative and delicious part of the meal.

Make your next gathering deliciously different by teaming a few salads as the star attraction. When selecting salads, check to see that the dressings have some variety. Also, try to imagine the color and texture of the salads beside one another. Look for a variety of greens and other vegetables as well as special ingredients — fruit, cheese, seafood, poultry, sausage, and interesting garnishes. Add hearty breads, muffins, crackers or bread sticks, and your prize dessert for a winning menu!

As a centerpiece for this party use beautiful heads of green lettuce — some curly, some red tipped — in handsome baskets. Or on a large wooden tray, arrange fresh green fruits and vegetables — cabbages, green peppers, cucumbers, green beans, brussels sprouts, asparagus, limes, green grapes. If you enjoy sending your guests home with party favors, assemble little trimmed baskets of fresh herbs. For an evening meal, try artichokes as candleholders for short chubby candles (votive).

For a very special touch serve a cold salad on frosty cold plates with chilled forks. Glass plates are ideal because they look icy, but any others can achieve the look.

When a delicious vegetable is part of a meal, it is usually devoured first. Vegetables, so easily, can be the highlight of a meal. But, often they are a disappointment because they are not prepared well or with much interest.

Although the supermarkets and farmers' markets abound with beautiful seasonal varieties, in menu planning the decision about the vegetables is often the biggest challenge. Cook fresh vegetables by simply steaming, boiling, sautéing, or microwaving. Most are packed with flavor and taste wonderful with a minimum of additions. Faster yet are raw vegetables. They taste good and are good for you. For a refreshing change, try unfamiliar vegetables and substitute your favorites in some of your tried-and-true standby recipes. Vegetables can add interest to your menus and be the highlight of your meals!

Treat vegetables with imagination and enthusiasm! For contrasting flavors and textures add nuts, seeds, water chestnuts, chopped herbs, dry bread crumbs, currants or freshly grated cheese.

Fiesta Bowl Salad

PREPARATION TIME: *30 minutes plus 2 hours chilling time*
YIELD: *6 – 8 servings*

2 small or 1 large head cauliflower	1. Trim cauliflower, break into small flowerets. Blanch in boiling water 10 minutes. Drain immediately, and fill pot with cold water to cover flowerets. Add 1 or 2 ice cubes to insure water remains cool. Let set for 5 minutes.
½ cup red wine vinegar	
½ cup olive oil	
1 tablespoon garlic salt	
½ cup crumbled blue cheese	2. Combine the red wine vinegar, olive oil, garlic salt, and crumbled blue cheese. Whisk together to blend thoroughly. Let set while assembling salad.
1 small red Bell pepper, cut into strips	
1 small green Bell pepper, cut into strips	3. Place cauliflower (drained), peppers, and onion in a medium sized glass or plastic salad bowl. Pour dressing over salad, sprinkle with pepper and toss gently to coat well. Chill for a few hours, stir occasionally. Serve slightly chilled.
1 red onion sliced thin	

"This colorful salad is great for tailgates or TV game parties. Tastes better as it sets."

Celeste Sychterz Salvaggio '82 Aersp

Decreasing fat can be accomplished by using ¼ cup olive oil and ¼ cup water and less blue cheese. You will still have the "taste" of the cheese, but without the fat and calories. Garlic powder is also preferable to garlic salt.

Spring Break Salad

PREPARATION TIME: *15 minutes*
YIELD: *5 – 7 servings*

1 **head leaf lettuce**

A few young raddichio leaves, (more greenish than red)

1 **handful mixed alfalfa and radish sprouts**

1. Prepare the greens carefully. (You might find the sprouts pre-mixed at your grocery store.)

2. Arrange in individual bowls or salad plates. Mix dressing in a separate bottle or jar and add it to salad servings just before eating. Best served just slightly cooler than room temperature.

DRESSING

¼ **cup fresh lemon juice**

1 **small clove garlic, crushed**

1½ **teaspoons grated lemon peel**

2 **teaspoons fresh or 1 teaspoon dried thyme**

⅓ **cup chopped parsley**

1½ **teaspoons sugar (more if lemons are extremely tart)**

¾ **cup cold-pressed safflower oil**

½ **teaspoon salt**

Generous shakes of fresh ground pepper or lemon-pepper

1. Combine all ingredients in a jar and shake well.

A great salad solution to the problem of never finding fresh, ripe tomatoes. Resist the urge to toss in additonal vegetables, as this would alter the delicate flavor balance.

Cathy Mix Campbell '83 GnAS

Turner Salad LeMont

PREPARATION TIME: *30 minutes plus chilling time for dressing*
YIELD: *6 servings*

SALAD

4 cups small broccoli flowerets, blanched if desired

1 cup raisins

1 cup sliced mushrooms

½ cup chopped red onion

6 slices of bacon, cooked until crisp and crumbled

Salt and pepper, to taste

1. In a large bowl combine the broccoli, raisins, mushrooms, onion and bacon. Pour the dressing over the mixture. Toss salad well. Add salt and pepper to taste.

DRESSING

1 large whole egg

1 large egg yolk

½ cup sugar

½ teaspoon dry mustard

1½ teaspoons cornstarch

¼ cup distilled white vinegar

¼ cup water

¼ teaspoon salt

2 tablespoons unsalted butter

½ cup mayonnaise

1. In a small bowl whisk together the whole egg, egg yolk, sugar, mustard, and cornstarch.

2. In a saucepan combine vinegar, water and salt; bring to a boil over moderate heat.

3. Whisk in egg mixture and cook. Whisk for 1 minute, or until thickened. Remove from heat and whisk in butter.

4. Whisk in mayonnaise. Cover and chill the dressing.

Marcia Hutter Fehl '74 MEd HEEd

Low-calorie mayonnaise, non-fat yogurt or soft tofu (creamed in food processor) are nice substitutes for mayonnaise, decreasing fat and calories.

Artichoke Salad

PREPARATION TIME: *30 minutes plus 24 hours chilling time*
YIELD: *10 – 12 servings*

2 (14 ounce) cans artichoke hearts, drained and cut in small pieces

1 (19 ounce) can chick-peas, drained and rinsed

2 (4 ounce) jars marinated mushrooms, cut up

Chopped garlic, to taste

½ cup dried or fresh parsley

Salt and pepper, to taste

2 tablespoons olive oil

1 tablespoon vinegar

Capers (optional)

1. In a two quart container mix all ingredients together and marinate in refrigerator for 24 hours before serving. Marinating is vital for taste.

Louise Inserra Lockwood '50 Ed

93

Mandarin Salad

PREPARATION TIME: *20 minutes*
YIELD: *4 – 6 servings*

SALAD

- ¼ **cup sliced almonds**
- 1 **tablespoon plus 1 teaspoon sugar**
- ¼ **head lettuce**
- ¼ **head romaine**
- 2 **green onions including tops, thinly sliced**
- 1 **cup chopped celery**
- 1 **(11 ounce) can mandarin oranges, drained**

1. Cook almonds in sugar over low heat. Stir constantly until sugar melts and almonds are coated. Cool and break apart. Store at room temperature.

2. Tear head lettuce and romaine into bite-sized pieces (about 4 cups).

3. Place greens, green onions and celery in plastic bag and refrigerate.

4. Five minutes before serving pour dressing into bag; add orange segments. Fasten bag and shake until greens and oranges are well coated.

5. Add almonds and shake. Serve.

DRESSING

- ½ **teaspoon salt**
- **Dash of pepper**
- 2 **tablespoons sugar**
- 2 **tablespoons vinegar**
- ¼ **cup salad oil**
- **Dash red pepper sauce**
- 1 **tablespoon snipped parsley**

1. Shake dressing ingredients in tightly covered jar; refrigerate.

Can do ahead.

Christine Young Boyer '68 Engl

Broccoli and Mushroom Salad

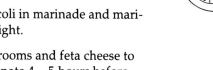

PREPARATION TIME: *30 minutes plus overnight and 4 – 5 hours marinating time*
YIELD: *20 servings*

3 bunches broccoli, cleaned and cut up

1¼ pounds mushrooms, sliced

4 ounces feta cheese, crumbled

MARINADE

1 cup olive oil

¾ cup cider vinegar

3 tablespoons Dijon mustard

9 tablespoons brown sugar

3 cloves garlic, pressed

3 teaspoons salt

Pepper, to taste

1. Mix marinade ingredients together.

2. Place broccoli in marinade and marinate overnight.

3. Add mushrooms and feta cheese to salad. Marinate 4 – 5 hours before serving.

Jayne Rider Kelly '68 CSB

This marinade would be just as tasty with ½ cup olive oil and ½ cup water and less salt.

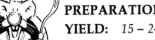

Lion Layered Salad

PREPARATION TIME: *30 minutes plus 8 – 12 hours chilling time*
YIELD: *15 – 24 servings*

1 **head lettuce**
1 **cup diced celery**
4 **hard-boiled eggs, sliced**
1 **(10 ounce) package frozen peas, uncooked**
½ **cup sliced green peppers**
1 **medium sweet onion, sliced**
8 **slices bacon, cooked and diced**
2 **tablespoons sugar**
2 **cups mayonnaise**
4 **ounces grated Cheddar cheese**

1. Tear lettuce into bite-size pieces and put into bottom of 9 × 13-inch glass dish or deep bowl.

2. Layer celery, eggs, peas, peppers, onion and bacon in order given.

3. In separate bowl mix sugar with mayonnaise and spread over top of salad like a frosting.

4. Top with cheese, cover and refrigerate 8 – 12 hours. Seal tightly and it will keep for a week.

Rosalie A. Radio
Gregory J. Radio '69 PM, '73 MD Med

To vary, use your creativity and foods you like. To decrease cholesterol, omit eggs and bacon, and use an alternative to mayonnaise, such as non-fat yogurt.

Spinach Salad

PREPARATION TIME: *15 minutes*
YIELD: *8 servings*

2 (8 ounce) packages fresh spinach, washed and well drained

½ pound lean bacon, fried crisp

2 hard-cooked eggs, coarsely chopped

5 scallions, minced

¾ cup garlic croutons

1. Remove stems from spinach.

2. Tear leaves into bite-size pieces.

3. Place spinach in salad bowl.

4. Crumble bacon and arrange eggs, scallions and croutons over spinach.

DRESSING

½ cup mayonnaise

2 teaspoons mustard

¼ cup lemon juice

½ cup olive or salad oil

1 tablespoon tarragon vinegar

⅛ teaspoon sugar

1 clove garlic, crushed

Salt and pepper to taste

1. Combine all ingredients in jar with lid and mix well.

2. Prior to serving pour dressing over salad and toss lightly.

Carolyn Rice Kirkpatrick '49 A&L
Henry H. Kirkpatrick '48 IE

Zesty Spring Salad

PREPARATION TIME: *20 minutes plus chilling time*
YIELD: *7 – 10 servings*

1 **(16 ounce) box spring noodles**	1. Cook spring noodles according to directions on box.
½ **pound hard salami, cubed**	
½ **pound sharp Cheddar cheese, cubed**	2. Combine remaining ingredients with cooked noodles. Place in large salad bowl. Chill.
1 **cucumber, sliced and quartered**	
1 **medium red onion, chopped**	
1 **(7 ounce) jar green olives**	
1 **(6 ounce) can black olives**	
2 **fresh tomatoes, wedged**	
1 **medium green pepper, chopped**	
1 **(16 ounce) jar zesty Italian dressing**	

Mary Lea Bowers

During this century, Penn State researchers in agriculture have developed more than 180 varieties of plants.

Bean Sprout Salad

PREPARATION TIME: *20 minutes*
YIELD: *4 – 6 servings*

2 **medium tomatoes, cut in wedges**

1 **cucumber, skin scored and thinly sliced**

1 **avocado, pared and sliced**

2 – 3 **cups fresh bean sprouts**

Salad greens

½ **cup salad oil**

2 **tablespoons fresh lemon or lime juice**

2 **tablespoons vinegar**

¾ **teaspoon salt**

¼ **teaspoon sugar**

½ **teaspoon dry mustard**

Dash of pepper

3 **strips bacon, cooked and crumbled**

1. Combine tomato wedges, cucumber slices, avocado slices and bean sprouts in salad bowl.

2. Garnish edge of bowl with salad greens.

3. Just before serving, mix oil, lemon or lime juice, vinegar, salt, sugar, dry mustard and pepper together.

4. Pour this mixture over salad and sprinkle with bacon bits.

Marye Hartzell Settles '51 A&L

Bean sprouts are such a healthy food! Children and adults alike usually enjoy the fun of growing their own. Instructions abound for growing sprouts in jars, "sprouters" or special linen bags.

Carrot and Three Bean Salad

PREPARATION TIME: *15 minutes plus chilling time*

YIELD: *10 servings*

½ cup white vinegar

Low-calorie or no-calorie sweetener equal to ½ cup sugar

2 tablespoons salad oil

1 teaspoon salt

1 teaspoon dry mustard

1 (15 ounce) can kidney beans

1 (15 ounce) can green beans

1 (15 ounce) can wax beans

1 (15 ounce) can sliced or baby carrots

1 small onion, sliced thin

¼ cup chopped green pepper

¼ cup chopped celery

2 tablespoons parsley

1. Combine the vinegar, sweetener, salad oil, salt and mustard in jar with lid. Shake well.

2. Drain canned vegetables. Pour dressing over vegetables.

3. Add onion, green pepper, celery and parsley. Stir carefully to mix.

4. Refrigerate several hours to chill. Overnight if possible.

Martha Worthington Harris '54 HEc

Red Cabbage Slaw

PREPARATION TIME: *20 minutes*
YIELD: *6 – 8 servings*

1 **pound red cabbage, shredded**

3 **large carrots, grated**

2 **apples, chopped**

½ **cup raisins**

2 **celery stalks, chopped**

½ **cup alfalfa sprouts**

¼ **cup chopped parsley**

½ **cup sunflower seeds**

1. In a large salad bowl combine all ingredients, except sunflower seeds, and mix well.

DRESSING

¼ **cup lemon juice**

1 **tablespoon honey**

1 **tablespoon grated onion**

2 **teaspoons prepared mustard**

½ **cup safflower oil**

1. Whisk together dressing ingredients.

2. Pour dressing over salad and toss to mix.

3. Garnish by sprinkling sunflower seeds over salad.

Cleta K. Leinbach
Richard B. Leinbach '57 MEd, '78 PhD AEd

To decrease the need for sweeteners, eliminate the lemon juice and equivalent sweetener. They often tend to "balance each other" and aren't missed.

Special Chicken Salad

PREPARATION TIME: *1 hour 30 minutes*

YIELD: *8 servings*

3 cups diced cooked chicken, breasts only (skinned)

1½ cups diced celery

3 tablespoons lemon juice

1½ – 2 cups seedless green or red grapes (halved)

¾ cup chopped pecans

1 cup mayonnaise

¼ cup light cream

Pepper, to taste

1 teaspoon dry mustard

1 teaspoon mild curry

½ teaspoon powdered ginger

1. Combine chicken, celery and lemon juice. Chill at least one hour.

2. Add grapes and pecans.

3. Combine and mix the mayonnaise, cream, pepper, mustard, curry and ginger.

4. Pour over and mix with the chicken mixture.

5. Serve and enjoy.

Sally T. Woomert
Dale E. Woomert '49, '51 MS ME

To decrease fat, substitute non-fat yogurt for mayonnaise and skim milk for the cream.

Winter Fruit Salad

PREPARATION TIME: *10 minutes*
YIELD: *8 – 10 servings*

1½ cups pineapple juice

1 tablespoon sugar

¼ cup cornstarch

2 tablespoons fresh lemon juice

⅔ cup orange juice (not mandarin)

2 (20 ounce) cans pineapple chunks, drained

2 (11 ounce) cans mandarin oranges

4 medium apples, chopped

4 bananas, sliced

1. Mix pineapple juice, sugar, cornstarch, lemon juice and orange juice together. Bring to a boil. Stir constantly. Boil for 1 minute.

2. Pour dressing over pineapple chunks, mandarin oranges, apples and bananas.

Judi Stern Feldstein
Jay H. Feldstein '59 A&L

Unsweetened 100% pure fruit juices and fruits packed in water are the best buys for health.

Victory Mold

PREPARATION TIME: *30 minutes plus 3 hours chilling time*
YIELD: *10 – 12 servings*

1 (6 ounce) package lemon-flavored gelatin

½ cup boiling water

1 pint sour cream

1 (6 ounce) package cherry-flavored gelatin

½ cup boiling water

1 (16 ounce) can or jar of blueberries or blueberry pie filling

1. Dissolve lemon-flavored gelatin in ½ cup boiling water. Cool for a few minutes.

2. Add sour cream to gelatin and mix well. Pour into a 1-quart mold.

3. Refrigerate 3 hours or until very firm.

4. Dissolve cherry-flavored or any red gelatin in ½ cup boiling water. Cool for a few minutes.

5. Add undrained blueberries or pie filling to gelatin.

6. Pour on top of firm lemon and sour cream layer.

7. Refrigerate until serving time.

Dorothy Todaro
Mario F. Todaro '57, '75 MEd IAEd

Orange Salad

PREPARATION TIME: *10 minutes plus 4 hours chilling time*
YIELD: *4 – 6 servings*

1 (3 ounce) package apricot or orange gelatin

12 ounces cottage cheese

1 (11 ounce) can mandarin oranges, drained

1 (8¼ ounce) can crushed pineapple, drained

½ cup whipping cream

¼ cup powdered sugar

½ teaspoon vanilla

1. Sprinkle gelatin over cottage cheese. Add oranges, pineapple, and stir well.

2. Whip cream with powdered sugar and vanilla, fold into gelatin mixture. Cover and refrigerate for at least 4 hours.

Melinda Johnson

"Crush 'em Lion Salad"

PREPARATION TIME: *1 hour 10 minutes*
YIELD: *14 – 18 servings*

2 cups crushed unsalted pretzels

3 tablespoons sugar

¾ cup margarine, melted

8 ounces cream cheese

⅓ cup sugar

1 package Dream Whip topping

2 (3 ounce) packages strawberry gelatin

2 cups boiling water

2 (10 ounce) packages frozen strawberries

1. Combine pretzels and 3 tablespoons sugar in an 8-inch square baking dish.

2. Add melted margarine and mix completely.

3. Bake at 400° for 8 minutes.

4. Remove from oven and cool in refrigerator.

5. Mix cream cheese, ⅓ cup sugar, and dry whipped topping. Beat with an electric mixer until creamy. Spread cream cheese mixture over pretzel mixture, creating a layer effect.

6. Chill baking dish with pretzels and cream cheese mixture.

7. Mix boiling water with gelatin; add frozen strawberries. Refrigerate mixture for 10 minutes.

8. Spread strawberry mixture on top of cream cheese to make third layer. Cover with plastic wrap and refrigerate overnight.

"When people eat this salad they swear that the pretzels are nuts!"

Spray baking dish with a vegetable spray for easy removal. Cut salad with a knife, then remove pieces with a spatula.

Sharon Neff Ryba '80 2HFS

Apricot Delight

PREPARATION TIME: *30 minutes plus chilling time*
YIELD: *15 – 20 servings*

2 **(3 ounce) boxes apricot-flavored gelatin**

2 **cups hot water**

2 **cups cold water**

1 **(20 ounce) can crushed pineapple, drain, reserve juice**

2 **bananas, sliced**

2 **cups miniature marshmallows**

½ **cup reserved pineapple juice**

¾ **cup sugar**

1 **egg, beaten**

2 **tablespoons flour**

8 **ounces cream cheese, softened**

1 **envelope Dream Whip**

1 **(3½ ounce) can coconut**

1. Mix gelatin and hot water until gelatin dissolves. Add cold water. Stir. Let jell.

2. Add drained crushed pineapple, bananas and marshmallows. Stir together and place in a 9 × 13-inch pan.

3. In small saucepan combine pineapple juice, sugar, egg and flour. Cook until thick.

4. Remove from heat and add cream cheese. Mix until smooth and let cool.

5. Prepare whipped topping according to package instructions.

6. Fold whipped topping into cooled cream cheese mixture.

7. Spread mixture over jello mixture and sprinkle with coconut.

8. Chill until firm.

Jane R. Stoner

If you omit marshmallows in recipes, substitute 1 – 2 teaspoons vanilla for the same taste.

Baked Beans

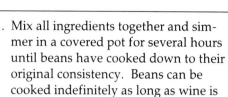

PREPARATION TIME: *5 – 7 hours*
YIELD: *10 – 12 servings*

5 (16 ounce) cans pork and beans

2 cups dry wine

1 cup dark brown sugar

1 cup orange or apple blossom honey

1 tablespoon ground bay leaf

1 tablespoon cracked pepper

1. Mix all ingredients together and simmer in a covered pot for several hours until beans have cooked down to their original consistency. Beans can be cooked indefinitely as long as wine is added after beans have cooked down.

"The longer they cook and the more wine you add, the better and more homemade the flavor. The recipe is authentic and original, a perfect pot to take on a picnic!"

Judy Vandergrift
James B. Vandergrift '64 BA

Try reducing the sugar by half. Use ½ cup brown sugar and ½ cup honey. Use vegetarian baked beans and you could make an easy meatless, low-fat entree or side dish.

Blue-White Day Bean Bake

PREPARATION TIME: *1 hour 15 minutes*
YIELD: *20 servings*

1 **pound bulk pork sausage**

1 **cup chopped onions**

1 **cup chopped celery**

1 **(3 pound 5¼ ounce) can pork and beans**

1 **(1 pound 6 ounce) can hot chili beans and gravy**

1 **(16 ounce) can cut wax beans, drained**

1 **(16 ounce) can cut green beans, drained**

1 **(16 ounce) can lima beans, drained**

1 **(10 ounce) can tomato soup**

1 **cup brown sugar**

1 **(6 ounce) can tomato paste**

3 – 4 **slices bacon, cooked and crumbled (optional)**

1. In a medium frying pan over medium heat, brown sausage, onions and celery, breaking sausage into chunks with a spoon or spatula as you cook. Drain off grease and put sausage mixture into large roasting pan.

2. Without draining, add the pork and beans and chili beans to roaster.

3. Add the drained wax, green and lima beans, tomato soup (undiluted), and brown sugar. Mix well.

4. Spread the tomato paste on top (will not cover entire pan) and sprinkle with the bacon, if desired. Place, uncovered, in oven.

5. Bake at 350° for one hour. Then stir through the tomato paste.

Can be transferred to crockpot to keep hot after baking.

Susan Beck Wilson '71 SecEd
Edward J. Wilson '70 Mktg

Million Dollar Beans

PREPARATION TIME: *1 hour 35 minutes*
YIELD: *8 servings*

½ **pound bacon chopped into small pieces**

2 **large onions, chopped**

½ **teaspoon dry mustard**

½ **cup vinegar**

1 **cup brown sugar**

1 **(16 ounce) can red kidney beans, drained**

1 **(16 ounce) can small lima beans, drained**

1 **(28 – 31 ounce) can pork and beans, undrained**

1. Fry bacon and onion together until onion is soft and bacon is beginning to brown. Do not pour off bacon grease.

2. Add mustard, vinegar and brown sugar. Simmer 20 minutes.

3. Place kidney beans, lima beans and pork and beans in a 2½-quart casserole dish.

4. Add bacon mixture to beans and stir.

5. Bake uncovered at 350° for 1 hour. Stir occasionally.

John A. Hauptman '49 IE

If you use cooked dry beans in recipes, soak and cook a large batch. Freeze in quantities needed for recipes like this.

Maryland Corn Pudding

PREPARATION TIME: *1 hour*

YIELD: *4 servings*

- 2 **cups corn, (frozen, canned or fresh)**
- 1 **tablespoon flour**
- 2 **tablespoons sugar**
- 2 **eggs**
- ¾ **teaspoon salt**
- ¾ **cup milk**
- ¼ **cup butter**

1. Combine all ingredients in a blender and mix for 10 seconds at high speed. Pour into a greased 1-quart baking dish.

2. Bake at 375° for 45 minutes.

Alice Raphel Linberg '78 MBA BA

Lone Star Paw-tatoes

PREPARATION TIME: *1 hour 30 minutes*
YIELD: *6 – 8 servings*

4	baking potatoes
2	tablespoons butter or margarine
¼	cup milk
1	cup grated Velveeta cheese
¾	cup chopped green onions
1	cup shredded Cheddar cheese
	Bacon bits, to taste
	Paprika
	Seasoned pepper, to taste

1. Bake potatoes in conventional oven about 1 hour. Cut in half lengthwise and scoop out the inside and place in bowl; reserve "shells."

2. Add butter or margarine and milk to potatoes in bowl; mix well.

3. Stir in Velveeta cheese and onions. Fill the potato "shells" with this mixture.

4. Sprinkle tops of potatoes with Cheddar cheese, bacon bits, paprika and seasoned pepper.

5. Bake at 350° for 15 minutes.

Can do everything ahead, except last 15 minutes of baking.

Susan Stone Applbaum '68 MA Spch
Ronald L. Applbaum '69 PhD Spch

Better-than-HUB Asparagus

PREPARATION TIME: *10 minutes plus 30 minutes standing time*
YIELD: *5 – 6 servings*

1 tablespoon soy sauce

¾ teaspoon ground ginger

1 clove garlic, crushed

1 pound asparagus

2 tablespoons salad oil

1. Combine soy sauce, ginger and garlic; mix well. Let stand 30 minutes.

2. Wash asparagus. Remove tough ends. Slant cut into 1-inch pieces.

3. In skillet or fry pan heat oil over high heat. Add sauce and asparagus. Stir fry 2 minutes; cover and steam until asparagus is tender (3 – 5 minutes). Serve at once.

"My husband liked the HUB asparagus. After we married, I found this recipe, slightly modified it, and he likes this even better."

Madeline Pecora Nugent '70 EKEd, '71 MEd Engl

Fresh ginger is wonderful to keep on hand. Peel, slice and store in a small bottle of sherry in the refrigerator. In a recipe, use equivalent amount of minced fresh ginger.

Lion Fodder

PREPARATION TIME: *20 minutes*
YIELD: *4 – 6 spears per serving*

4 – 6 **spears of asparagus per person**

    Coarse saltine crumbs

  1 **teaspoon Parmesan or Romano cheese, or both**

  1 **teaspoon butter**

    Pinch salt

    Pinch pepper

1. Tear foil to fit number of spears to be prepared. Place foil shiny side up. Lay asparagus on foil, add remainder of ingredients. Enclose in foil, making certain it is sealed completely.

2. Cook on grill for 15 – 20 minutes.

Can be refrigerated, after step 1, for 2 – 3 days and carries well in ice chest to be cooked at tailgate.

Alice C. Hipple

Sesame Green Beans and Mushrooms

PREPARATION TIME: *10 minutes*
YIELD: *5 – 6 servings*

1 (9 ounce) package frozen French-cut green beans

1 cup sliced fresh mushrooms

2 tablespoons butter or margarine

2 teaspoons sesame seed

1 teaspoon sugar

½ teaspoon salt

⅛ teaspoon pepper

1. Place beans in 1-quart microwave-safe casserole. Cover with lid.

2. Microwave on high for 3 – 4 minutes or until just about thawed. Stir to break beans apart.

3. Add mushrooms, cover.

4. Microwave on high for 2 – 2½ minutes or until mushrooms are tender. Drain.

5. Add butter, sesame seeds, sugar, salt and pepper.

6. Microwave on high for 2 – 2½ minutes or until butter is melted and vegetables are hot. Stir lightly to coat evenly.

Barbara Yingling

Garlic or onion powders often substitute well for salt.

Penn State is the world leader in research in the growth and processing of mushrooms.

Touchdown Curried Fruit Bake

PREPARATION TIME: *10 minutes plus 1 hour cooking time*
YIELD: *6 – 8 servings*

1 **(29 ounce) can peach halves or slices**

1 **(20 ounce) can pineapple chunks**

1 **(16 ounce) can pear halves**

1 **(4 ounce) jar maraschino cherries**

⅓ **cup butter or margarine**

¾ **cup light brown sugar**

4 **teaspoons curry powder**

1. Drain fruit, dry on a paper towel.

2. Arrange fruit in a 1½-quart casserole or shallow baking dish.

3. Melt butter or margarine, add brown sugar and curry.

4. Spoon over fruit.

5. Bake uncovered at 325° for one hour.

6. Reheat the next day at 350° for 30 minutes.

Louise C. Tarman

You can eliminate a few calories by using fruit packed in water and decreasing the sugar and butter by half.

Ed's Green Beans

PREPARATION TIME: *40 minutes*
YIELD: *4 – 6 servings*

⅓ cup chopped onion

2 tablespoons butter or margarine

2 tablespoons flour

1 teaspoon salt

¼ teaspoon pepper

1 cup sour cream

2 (16 ounce) cans French-style green beans, drained

1 cup shredded Cheddar cheese

1. In a skillet, sauté onions in butter until tender, but not browned. Remove from heat and stir in flour, salt, pepper and then sour cream. Return to heat, stir and cook for a minute or two until smooth and thick.

2. Stir in beans, mixing well. Place mixture in a greased 1½-quart casserole. Sprinkle cheese on top.

3. Bake at 350° for 15 – 20 minutes, until heated through and the cheese is lightly browned.

To prepare ahead, complete through step 2; cover and refrigerate. Increase baking time to about 30 minutes if casserole has been refrigerated.

As penny-counting graduate students, my husband and I frequently spent Saturday evenings playing bridge with another grad student and a faculty member, Ed Rosenstock, our friend and "mentor" from Exam Services. We would have dinner together first, and always had the same thing: strip steaks (which Ed brought, since he could afford to buy them!), tossed salad, green bean casserole, and brownies. The green bean casserole was the most important part of the meal, since it was Ed's favorite. There was never any left — Ed always finished off whatever was there. To this day, we still call this "Ed's Beans."

Katherine (Lani) Clark Bloomer '67 Engl, '76 MS FEHM

You can rinse canned vegetables several times to decrease the salt content. In this recipe, omitting the salt and using non-fat yogurt instead of sour cream will make it healthier.

116

Coed Casserole

PREPARATION TIME: *45 minutes*

YIELD: *6 – 8 servings*

2 pounds small yellow squash

¼ cup chopped onion

1 (10½ ounce) can cream of chicken soup

1 cup sour cream

1 cup shredded carrots

1 (8 ounce) package seasoned stuffing

½ cup melted margarine

1. Slice squash into ¼ inch slices. It is not necessary to peel squash unless the skin is unusually tough. Cook squash and onion for 5 minutes. Do not let squash get soft, just lightly steam. Drain completely.

2. Combine soup, sour cream and carrots. Fold in squash and onion mixture.

3. Mix the stuffing with the margarine. Spread half of the stuffing into a casserole, spoon the vegetable mixture on top, cover with the remaining stuffing.

4. Bake at 350° for 30 minutes.

Joyce Yundt Keiser '50 Psy

Making your own bread crumbs is easy. Cube leftover or stale whole grain breads and toast in oven. You can do this while baking another item. Add seasonings that you enjoy.

Eggplant Patrice

PREPARATION TIME: *1 hour*
YIELD: *4 – 6 servings*

1 small eggplant, peeled	1. Slice eggplant into ¼-inch slices.
4 medium tomatoes, sliced	2. Parboil eggplant until partially tender.
2 medium green peppers, chopped	3. Place a layer of eggplant in bottom of casserole, cover with a layer of sliced tomatoes.
2 medium onions, chopped	4. Fill spaces with a mixture of chopped green peppers and onions.
Salt	
Pepper	5. Sprinkle lightly with the salt, pepper, garlic salt and sugar.
Garlic salt	
Sugar	6. Add a layer of cheese.
¾ pound sharp Cheddar cheese, sliced ⅛-inch thick	7. Repeat layers until casserole is filled, ending with the cheese.

1. Slice eggplant into ¼-inch slices.

2. Parboil eggplant until partially tender.

3. Place a layer of eggplant in bottom of casserole, cover with a layer of sliced tomatoes.

4. Fill spaces with a mixture of chopped green peppers and onions.

5. Sprinkle lightly with the salt, pepper, garlic salt and sugar.

6. Add a layer of cheese.

7. Repeat layers until casserole is filled, ending with the cheese.

8. Cover and bake at 400° for 30 minutes.

9. Remove cover and reduce heat to 350° for 30 minutes.

Jayne Koskinas

This is an excellent way to cook eggplant! In recipes that call for eggplant to be fried, use this parboil method or broil until browned and turn over. Eggplant absorbs oil "like a sponge," so alternative methods of cooking are healthier.

Lion's Sweet Potato Casserole

PREPARATION TIME: *40 minutes*
YIELD: *5 – 7 servings*

3 **cups mashed sweet potatoes**

¾ **cup brown sugar**

1 **egg**

1 **teaspoon salt**

1 **teaspoon vanilla**

1 **teaspoon butternut flavoring**

4 **ounces evaporated milk**

¾ **cup coconut (optional)**

2 **tablespoons margarine**

½ **cup sugar**

3 **teaspoons chopped pecans**

½ **cup coconut (optional)**

2 **tablespoons margarine**

1. In a medium bowl mix sweet potatoes, brown sugar, egg, salt, vanilla, butternut flavoring, evaporated milk, coconut, and margarine together. Pour into a greased 1½-quart casserole.

2. Combine sugar and pecans; sprinkle over top of casserole.

3. Sprinkle with coconut and dot with margarine.

4. Bake at 325° for 15 minutes.

"Great color for a holiday dish. Wonderful with baked ham or turkey."

Robert L. Martin Family

In a hurry? Use vacuum-packed sweet potatoes. They have no added sweeteners. Since coconut is high in saturated fats, which contribute to heart disease, try a small amount of coconut, maybe ¼ cup, and add 1 teaspoon coconut extract for flavor.

Corn-Mushroom Bake

PREPARATION TIME: *1 hour 10 minutes*
YIELD: *6 – 8 servings*

¼ cup flour

1 (17 ounce) can creamed corn

3 ounces cream cheese, cubed

½ teaspoon onion salt

1 (17 ounce) can whole-kernel corn, drained

1 (4 ounce) can mushrooms, drained

½ cup shredded Swiss cheese

1½ cups soft bread crumbs

2 tablespoons butter or margarine, melted

1. In saucepan stir flour into cream style corn.

2. Add cream cheese and onion salt. Heat and stir until cream cheese melts.

3. Stir in whole kernel corn, mushrooms and Swiss cheese.

4. Pour mixture into a 2½-quart greased casserole.

5. Toss soft bread crumbs with melted butter or margarine.

6. Sprinkle crumbs on top of casserole.

7. Bake at 350° for 40 minutes or until heated through.

Must serve immediately.

Barbara Edwards Rudisill '84 MEd TC

120

Corn, Limas and Tomatoes à la Lion

PREPARATION TIME: *20 minutes plus 1 hour 10 minutes cooking time*
YIELD: *8 servings*

1 medium onion, chopped

1 green pepper, chopped

Salad oil

1 (16 ounce) can whole-kernel white corn, drained

1 (17 ounce) can lima beans, drained

1 (8 ounce) can tomato sauce

1 (16 ounce) can stewed tomatoes

1 tablespoon Worcestershire sauce

Salt, to taste

Pepper, to taste

Seasoned salt, to taste

4 slices bacon

1. Cook onion and green pepper in a little oil until tender.

2. Combine the onion, pepper, corn, limas, tomato sauce, tomatoes and seasonings in an 8 × 8-inch casserole.

3. Lay the bacon slices across the top.

4. Bake covered at 350° for 1 hour.

5. Uncover and bake an additional 10 minutes to crisp the bacon.

Lynda Saubel Matakovich '67 HEES
James G. Matakovich '73 EE

In recipes that call for vegetables to be sautéed in oil, you can always steam them in a basket or in a small amount of water to decrease fat.

Vegetable-Rice Casserole

PREPARATION TIME: *2 hours*
YIELD: *6 – 8 servings*

2 cups brown rice

2 tablespoons butter

2 large onions, chopped

4 tablespoons soy sauce

4 cups vegetable broth

½ teaspoon thyme

3 tablespoons peanut oil (other kinds of oil can be used)

2 garlic cloves, chopped

2 red peppers, cut into strips

1 bunch broccoli, cut into flowerets

1 head cauliflower, cut into flowerets

1 cup cashews

2 cups (8 ounces) shredded Cheddar cheese

1. In large pot mix rice with butter, 1 large chopped onion, soy sauce and vegetable broth (for convenience, dissolve 4 teaspoons dehydrated broth in 4 cups water). Cook until rice is done (approximately 50 minutes for brown rice).

2. Stir in thyme.

3. Heat oil in large skillet. Sauté second onion, with garlic and red peppers. Add broccoli and cauliflower to sauté (broccoli and cauliflower can be partly steamed first if softer vegetables are preferred).

4. Spoon rice into large baking dish or 2 medium-sized dishes. Pour vegetables on top.

5. Cover and bake at 350° for 10 minutes.

6. Remove lid and sprinkle with cashews. Mound Cheddar cheese around the edges and bake until cheese is melted.

"This is a very healthy and very delicious dairy recipe. I usually make it for large potluck dinners or to serve and freeze half for lunches or dinner. Other vegetables can be substituted."

Marci Mayer Eisen '79 IFS

Leftover brown rice can be frozen for a quick and convenient start on another recipe. Soy sauce and vegetable broth are available in the low-sodium varieties.

Broccoli-Rice Casserole

PREPARATION TIME: *1 hour*
YIELD: *4 – 6 servings*

1 cup rice

2 (10 ounce) packages frozen broccoli spears or cuts

2 (10¾ ounce) cans cream of chicken or cream of mushroom soup

1 small chopped onion

6 – 8 ounces Velveeta cheese

½ cup margarine

1. Cook rice and frozen broccoli separately (chop broccoli if using spears).

2. In medium saucepan heat soup, chopped onion, cheese and margarine.

3. Add rice and broccoli. Place in large casserole dish.

4. Bake at 350° for 30 – 35 minutes.

Diane Evans

Brown rice contains more fiber and vitamins than white.

Charleston Rice

PREPARATION TIME: *20 minutes plus 1 hour baking time*
YIELD: *8 servings as a side dish*

¾ cup chopped onion	1. In heavy skillet sauté onion, green pepper, mushrooms and celery in the butter.
⅓ cup chopped green pepper	
2 cups sliced fresh mushrooms	2. Remove vegetables to a large mixing bowl. Set aside.
½ cup chopped celery	
1½ tablespoons butter	3. In same skillet sauté sausage, breaking it into little pieces. Drain off fat, add sausage to mixing bowl with vegetables.
1 pound bulk pork sausage	
1 cup uncooked long-grained rice	4. Add the rice and minced parsley, stir thoroughly.
2 tablespoons minced parsley	
2 cups hot chicken stock	5. Stir in hot chicken stock.

6. Pour into lightly greased 2½-quart casserole with lid.

7. Cover and bake at 350° for 30 minutes.

8. Remove from oven and stir gently.

9. Replace cover and bake an additional 30 minutes.

"A nice accompaniment to roast pheasant or Cornish game hens."

Lyn Kennedy

Parsley freezes well for use in recipes. Chop and spread on a cookie sheet. Freeze several hours. Store in boxes or a plastic bag for quick accessibility.

Helpful Salad Hints

For buffet service, it is better to underdress your salads, because dressings tend to run into other foods on the same plate. Offer handsome cruets of salad dressing on a pretty plate beside the salad bowl.

Leave space on the buffet beside each serving bowl because your guests might need to set down their plates while serving themselves.

Salads that contain fruit and/or gelatin can double as a dessert for brunch or a light luncheon. Apricot Delight with fruit marshmallows and coconut or the "Crush 'em Lion Salad" with berries, cream cheese and unsalted pretzels make delicious "dessert" salads!

Try this combination of salads as the main attraction of your next gathering:

Special Chicken Salad

Artichoke Salad

Red Cabbage Slaw

with

Chilled Bowl of Fresh Greens

Entrees

Using themes for entertaining can turn a little supper party into a memorable event! The Homecoming theme could be used to set the stage to host a TV game party. A recent one was "Discover at Penn State . . . A Whole New World!" That in itself suggests menu ideas from around the world, as well as a menu rich in Penn State pride: a mushroom dish that boasts of Penn State's mushroom technology and cones of Keeney Beaney chocolate or Peachy Paterno that are tasty reminders of the Creamery's latest flavors.

To celebrate the publication of **Cookin' With The Lion**, host a party! Whether you submitted a recipe, tested and tasted recipes, or simply appreciate them, this is the ideal time to gather your Penn State friends around your table. Go Penn State all the way! Invite them on Penn State note paper. Offer Penn State mints, available at the Penn State Book Store. Stretch your imagination to adapt what you already have at home to a Penn State theme. Or choose your theme from an idea on these pages . . . perhaps a picnic reminiscent of lazy afternoons spent at Whipple's Dam.

Do your flowers in elegant arrangements or in a casual one with wildflowers. Use the prettiest blue and white flowers available in your yard or at the florist.

Your invitations might read:

To celebrate the publication
of
Cookin' With The Lion,
and to
Enjoy the spirit of Penn State,
Please join us to dine with the Lion.

When You Entertain
Suggestions for Successful Menu Planning

1. Consider your theme. Today's busy hosts and hostesses find that even the simplest theme adds more fun and helps one select special foods for a particular meal.

2. In any meal plan a few dishes that are not overly rich.

3. Be aware of cold weather and warm weather appetite appeal. A hearty stew on a cold evening is as welcome as a cold seafood salad for a spring luncheon.

4. Choose dishes that can wait a few minutes, if necessary, before being served. You, and not the food, need to be in control of the party. Allow only one dish requiring last-minute preparation.

5. Remember the value of eye appeal!

Lion's Paw Ribs

PREPARATION TIME: *2 hours 30 minutes*
YIELD: *4 – 6 servings*

7 – 8 **pounds pork ribs**

1 **cup flour**

1 **tablespoon paprika**

1½ **teaspoons minced garlic**

¼ **teaspoon pepper**

2 **cups chili sauce**

½ **cup minced onion**

2 **tablespoons brown sugar**

2 **tablespoons vinegar**

2 **tablespoons dry mustard**

¾ **teaspoon tabasco sauce**

½ **teaspoon Worcestershire sauce**

1. Mix flour with paprika, garlic and pepper. Shake ribs in bag with flour mixture to coat ribs. Arrange ribs in shallow baking pan.

2. Bake at 325° for 1½ hours.

3. While ribs are baking, combine chili sauce, onion, sugar, vinegar, mustard, tabasco sauce, and Worcestershire sauce in pan and bring to a boil. Simmer on low heat for 15 minutes.

4. Prepare charcoal grill. Remove ribs from oven, baste with sauce and grill until crisp.

Will Zimmerman

Peach-Glazed Spareribs

PREPARATION TIME: *10 minutes plus 1 hour baking time*
YIELD: *4 servings*

½ cup brown sugar

¼ cup ketchup

¼ cup vinegar

1 (16 ounce) can peaches, drained

1 clove garlic

2 tablespoons soy sauce

1 teaspoon sage

1 teaspoon ginger

3 pounds spareribs

1. Place all ingredients, except spareribs, in blender. Blend until smooth.

2. Place ribs in pan and pour half of the glaze over them.

3. Bake at 350° for 45 minutes.

4. Pour remaining half of the glaze over ribs and bake for another 15 minutes.

Kristina Volpe Focht '82 Acctg

Roast Loin Of Pork

PREPARATION TIME: *3 hours*
YIELD: *8 – 10 servings*

6 **pounds pork loin**

Salt and pepper to taste

½ **teaspoon rosemary**

2 **cups chopped onions**

2 **cups chopped celery**

2 **cups chopped carrots**

½ **cup flour**

1 **quart chicken stock**

1. Place pork in greased roasting pan and rub surface of meat with salt, pepper and rosemary.

2. Place fat side up and roast at 350° for one hour.

3. Turn roast to assure browning on both sides, then add vegetables and continue roasting another hour. When done remove meat and vegetables from pan and keep warm.

4. Pour off ⅓ cup fat into sauce pan and add flour to make roux. Cook until lightly brown.

5. Place pan in which meat was roasted on stove and add chicken stock. Scrape pan to loosen brown particles, simmer 20 minutes, and strain. Add strained stock to roux, stir until thick and smooth. Strain again through fine sieve, and adjust seasoning.

Ralph B. Evans '57 HA

Use a rack so the fat drains off as the meat cooks.

Lion's Loins

PREPARATION TIME: *30 minutes plus 30 minutes marinating time*
YIELD: *4 servings*

2 garlic cloves, crushed

1 teaspoon brown sugar

3 tablespoons soy sauce

4 pork loin chops

1. Combine garlic, brown sugar and soy sauce in small bowl.

2. Brush chops well with marinade. Cover and set aside for at least 30 minutes. Brush occasionally with marinade.

3. Grill 8 – 10 minutes on each side. Brush chops with marinade and grill an additional 10 – 12 minutes, brush occasionally with marinade until done.

Mary Ellen Dunn Lowe '76 Hist

Cutting all visible fat from beef and pork helps to decrease fat and calories. Try this marinade with a pork loin, trimmed of all visible fat.

"Roarin', Scorin' Sausage & Kraut"

PREPARATION TIME: *45 minutes*
YIELD: *4 – 6 servings*

2 (16 ounce) cans sauerkraut

1 small yellow delicious apple

1 teaspoon celery seed

6 – 12 ounces of beer

1½ – 2 pounds smoked sausage

1. In a medium Dutch oven or covered pot add sauerkraut (do not drain). Dice and add apple, celery seed and beer; stir.

2. Cut sausage into bite size chunks, add to above mixture and stir until throughly mixed. Cook on low heat, stirring occasionally.

3. Serve with salad, rolls and beverage.

Kathi A. Hicks
Gary L. Hicks '82 BLog

Italian Sausage-Zucchini Casserole

PREPARATION TIME: *1 hour*
YIELD: *2 – 3 servings*

3 cups zucchini, cut into cubes

½ pound Italian sausage, regular or hot

¼ cup finely chopped onion

½ cup fine cracker crumbs

2 eggs, slightly beaten

¼ teaspoon ground thyme

¼ teaspoon oregano

½ cup grated Parmesan cheese

1. Steam zucchini until tender, but crisp. Drain.

2. Cook sausage and onion together until sausage loses all pinkness and onions are translucent. Drain well.

3. Combine zucchini, sausage, onions, cracker crumbs, eggs, thyme, oregano and ¼ cup of the cheese.

4. Pour into a greased 2-quart casserole. Top with remaining cheese.

5. Bake at 350° until brown, about 30 – 35 minutes.

Can do zucchini, sausage and onions in microwave.

Nancy Saylor Gamble '52 HEc, '55 MEd CDFR
Glenn W. Gamble '51, '55 MEd AgEd, '59 DEd CnEd

Glazed Ham Loaf

PREPARATION TIME: *15 minutes plus 1 hour 15 minutes baking time*
YIELD: *6 servings*

1 **pound smoked ham, ground**

¼ **pound pork butt, ground**

¼ **pound veal, ground**

2 **eggs**

½ **cup milk**

¾ **cup bread crumbs**

½ **cup brown sugar**

½ **cup chili sauce**

1. Mix the meats, eggs, milk and bread crumbs together until well blended.

2. Form into a loaf and place in a loaf pan.

3. Bake ham loaf at 325° for 1 hour.

4. While ham loaf is baking mix brown sugar and chili sauce together. Simmer over low heat.

5. Pour sauce over ham loaf.

6. Bake at 350° for an additional 15 minutes.

If plain ham loaf is desired, omit the brown sugar and chili sauce glaze and serve the meat with mustard sauce. Delicious served hot or cold.

Marion F. Shetter

Mighty Lion Meatloaf

PREPARATION TIME: *2 hours 15 minutes*

YIELD: *4 – 6 servings*

2 **pounds ground beef**

½ **cup chopped onion**

½ **teaspoon salt**

1 **egg**

¼ **teaspoon pepper**

2 **cups cracker crumbs**

1 **(10¾ ounce) can vegetable soup**

1. Mix all ingredients together in a large bowl. Shape into one large loaf or several individual loaves.

2. Bake covered at 350° for two hours.

3. Add water to pan before covering. Remove cover for last 30 minutes of cooking to brown top.

Georgeann Laughman '82 Micrb

A low sodium "convenience" soup can be substituted, in this recipe.

Mexican Fiesta

PREPARATION TIME: *3 hours*
YIELD: *14 – 18 servings*

4 pounds ground beef

3 onions, chopped

2 (28 ounce) cans peeled tomatoes

3 (8 ounce) cans tomato sauce

2 (6 ounce) cans tomato paste

3 tablespoons chili powder

2 tablespoons garlic powder

1 (28 ounce) can ranch-style beans, not drained

2 large onions, sliced in rings

1 pound grated Cheddar cheese

1 head lettuce, chopped

4 tomatoes, diced

1 cup chopped green olives

12 ounces mushrooms, sliced

Chopped avocado (optional)

2 (16 ounce) containers sour cream

2 (16 ounce) bags corn chips

1. In a large skillet brown ground beef and onions. Drain.

2. Add peeled tomatoes, tomato sauce, tomato paste, chili powder, garlic powder and beans; simmer for 2 hours.

3. In separate bowls serve the sliced onions, Cheddar cheese, lettuce, tomatoes, olives, mushrooms, avocado and sour cream.

4. Place generous handfuls of corn chips on each plate, spoon meat sauce over chips and top with any or all other ingredients, ending with sour cream.

Barbara Black Huster
Dwight A. Huster '75 MBA BA

"Roaring Good" Enchilada Casserole

PREPARATION TIME: *30 minutes*
YIELD: *4 servings*

1 **pound ground beef**

1 – 2 **(1.25 ounce) packages dry chili mix**

4 **cups tomato juice or water**

6 **flour tortillas**

½ **head lettuce, chopped**

1 **tomato, chopped**

1 **medium onion, chopped**

¾ **cup grated longhorn cheese**

1. Over medium heat in a large skillet slowly brown ground beef.

2. Add chili mix and tomato juice or water and simmer, covered for about 10 minutes.

3. Dip tortillas, one at a time, in the sauce and line a 9 × 13-inch glass dish with 3 of them.

4. Top tortillas with half of the chopped vegetables, cheese, and meat sauce. Add another layer of dipped tortillas and repeat layering with vegetables, cheese, and meat sauce.

5. Bake at 375° for 5 – 10 minutes or until cheese is melted and everything is heated.

Jean N. Hoke
Donald E. Hoke '58 2DDT

Penn State has the largest college food service operation in the United States.

Vicki's Fiesta Casserole

PREPARATION TIME: *40 minutes*
YIELD: *6 – 8 servings*

1½ pounds ground beef

1 medium onion, chopped

Salt and pepper, to taste

1 (8 ounce) can tomato sauce

12 ounces small curd cottage cheese

1 (4 ounce) can chopped green chilies

6 ounces grated mozzarella cheese

1 (6 ounce) package tortilla chips

1. Brown beef with the onion. Drain off grease.

2. Add salt and pepper to taste. Add tomato sauce and heat until warm.

3. Stir chilies into cottage cheese. Mix well.

4. Layer in a 9 × 13-inch pan the following, in the order given: tortilla chips, beef mixture, cottage cheese mixture and mozzarella cheese.

5. Bake at 350° for 20 minutes or microwave, covered, at medium to medium-high power for 12 minutes.

6. Garnish with additional chips standing on edge.

Jeanette Olach Janota '64 MS SPA, '86 MA Engls

Lean ground beef and low-fat cottage cheese would help to decrease the fat.

Nittany Roar Casserole

PREPARATION TIME: *30 minutes*
YIELD: *6 servings*

1 **pound ground beef**	1. Brown meat in olive oil.
1 **tablespoon olive oil**	2. Add onions; cook until tender.
¾ **cup finely chopped onion**	3. Stir in salt, pepper, garlic powder, thyme, oregano, bay leaf, tomatoes, soup, rice and half of the sliced olives. Bring to a boil.
1½ **teaspoons salt**	
Dash of pepper	
⅛ **teaspoon garlic powder**	4. Reduce heat and simmer 5 minutes.
⅛ **teaspoon thyme**	5. Spoon into 2-quart baking dish and top with cheese.
⅛ **teaspoon oregano**	
½ **small bay leaf**	6. Broil until cheese melts. Garnish with remaining olives.
1 **(16 ounce) can tomatoes**	
1 **(10½ ounce) can cream of mushroom soup**	
1 **cup instant rice, uncooked**	
6 **stuffed olives, sliced**	
2 – 3 **slices American cheese, cut into ½-inch strips**	

Joan Hickerson Stoeckinger '57 Journ

Sweet-Sour Meatballs with Vegetables

PREPARATION TIME: *1 hour*
YIELD: *12 – 15 servings*

MEATBALLS

2 pounds ground beef

1 cup bread crumbs

2 eggs

3 tablespoons soy sauce

¼ cup onion flakes or fresh grated onion

1 teaspoon salt

Dash garlic

Dash tabasco

Dash nutmeg

1. Mix all ingredients well and form into 1-inch diameter meatballs.

2. Brown in skillet or bake at 350° for 15 minutes.

3. While meatballs are cooking prepare sauce.

SAUCE

1 cup pineapple juice (drained from can of pineapple)

2 cups white vinegar

½ cup brown sugar

1 cup white sugar

4 tablespoons cornstarch

½ cup soy sauce

1. Combine all ingredients in a 2-quart saucepan and cook until thickened, about 10 – 15 minutes.

VEGETABLES

6 – 8 celery stalks

2 – 4 onions

2 – 4 green peppers

6 – 8 carrots

½ – 1 head cauliflower

1 large bunch broccoli

1 (16 ounce) can chunk pineapple, drained

1 (4 ounce) jar maraschino cherries

1. Cut celery, onions, green peppers, carrots, cauliflower and broccoli into fairly large bite-size chunks.

2. Parboil or microwave the carrots, cauliflower and broccoli until softened slightly.

3. Place meatballs in 6-quart pan or Dutch oven and pour sauce over them. Add all the vegetables and fruit, stir to mix. Serve warm or cold.

Linda Whitlock Werner
Harry T. Werner '74 SoW

Easy Skillet Stroganoff

PREPARATION TIME: *30 minutes*
YIELD: *4 – 5 servings*

1 **pound ground beef**

1 **medium onion, chopped**

1 **(10¾ ounce) can cream of mushroom soup**

1 **cup sour cream**

1 **(10¾ ounce) can beef broth**

3 **cups uncooked medium egg noodles**

½ **cup water**

1. In skillet, brown beef and cook onion until tender. Stir to separate meat; drain off fat.

2. Blend in mushroom soup and sour cream; add remaining ingredients. Bring to boil.

3. Cover and cook over low heat 10 minutes or until noodles are done. Stir often.

Kathleen Radabaugh Morris '76 IFS

Varying the types of noodles in recipes like this changes the appearance each time. Try a combination of whole wheat and spinach "flats" instead of white egg noodles.

Penna. Golden Mushroom Beef

PREPARATION TIME: *3 hours 15 minutes*
YIELD: *4 – 6 servings*

½ **cup wine, your choice**

1 **(10¾ ounce) can golden mushroom soup**

2 **pounds sirloin beef, cut into squares**

1. Combine wine, mushroom soup, beef in a buttered 1-quart casserole or baking dish.

2. Cover and bake at 250° for 3 hours.

G. Magdalene Hitchcock '26 HEc

Fullback Flank Steak

PREPARATION TIME: *20 minutes*
YIELD: *4 – 6 servings*

2 **cloves garlic, crushed**

4 **tablespoons soy sauce**

2 **tablespoons tomato paste**

2 **tablespoons peanut oil**

1 **teaspoon cracked pepper**

1 **teaspoon oregano**

2 **pounds flank steak**

1. In large bowl combine garlic, soy sauce, tomato paste, peanut oil, pepper, and oregano.

2. Rub steak with oil mixture and broil under very hot heat or over very hot coals for 5 minutes on each side.

3. To serve, carve on the diagonal.

Easy.

Diane Damweber Voit '72 Advt

California Teriyaki Flank Steak

PREPARATION TIME: *40 minutes plus 6 hours marinating time*
YIELD: *6 servings*

⅓ cup soy sauce

¼ teaspoon black pepper

¼ cup salad oil

2 medium garlic cloves, minced

2 tablespoons honey

2 tablespoons red wine vinegar

1 tablespoon fresh lime juice

1 tablespoon grated onion

2 teaspoons fresh grated ginger root

¼ cup dry red wine

2 pounds flank steak

1. Blend all ingredients except flank steak and mix well.

2. Pour sauce over flank steak. Marinate in shallow pan at least 6 hours, or overnight for the best results. The first hour marinate at room temperature and then refrigerate.

3. Barbecue over hot coals, no more than 6 minutes per side, basting frequently with sauce.

4. Slice across grain in very thin slices.

"This recipe uses less soy sauce and sugar than traditional teriyaki. Spices make up the flavor gap. Flank steak must be served rare to be its best."

Deborah Diehl Loeffler
Capt. Stephen R. Loeffler '68 Fin

Happy Valley Broil

PREPARATION TIME: *1 hour plus 12 hours marinating time*
YIELD: *4 – 6 servings*

1 – 1½ **pounds flank steak**

2 **tablespoons sherry**

2 **tablespoons soy sauce**

1 **tablespoon honey**

¼ **teaspoon garlic powder**

1 **tablespoon sugar**

1 **teaspoon salt**

⅛ **teaspoon pepper**

1. Poke holes in steak with fork. Combine remaining ingredients and spread over steak. Marinate for at least 10 hours, or overnight, in refrigerator. Turn steak over in marinade occasionally.

2. Remove steak from marinade and grill on a barbecue (or broil in oven) until done. To serve, slice in thin strips (about ¼-inch) against grain. Marinade can be heated and used as a dipping sauce for meat.

Veronica Gambone Jones '73 PM, '77 MD Med

Try this good-tasting marinade with skinned chicken or tofu for great taste and less fat.

Beef Stroganoff

PREPARATION TIME: *30 minutes plus 1 hour cooking time*
YIELD: *4 – 6 servings*

1 **pound round steak, sliced thin**

Flour

2 **tablespoons shortening**

½ **cup chopped onion**

1 **clove garlic, minced**

1 **(6 ounce) can sliced mushrooms**

1 **cup sour cream**

1 **(10½ ounce) can tomato soup**

1 **tablespoon Worcestershire sauce**

6 – 8 **drops tabasco sauce**

½ **teaspoon salt**

⅛ **teaspoon pepper**

Fluffy rice

Parmesan cheese

1. Dip meat in flour and brown in hot shortening over medium heat.

2. Add onion, garlic and mushrooms; stir until onion is cooked.

3. Combine sour cream, tomato soup, Worcestershire sauce, tabasco sauce, salt and pepper. Pour over meat and simmer until meat is tender, about one hour.

4. Serve over fluffy rice and pass the Parmesan cheese.

"This can be tripled (or more) to serve a crowd. Can be made ahead of time and reheated in a slow oven (300°) until serving time."

Bert Douthett Goerder '41 HEc

Savory Garden Goulash

PREPARATION TIME: *1 hour 45 minutes*
YIELD: *8 large servings*

¾ cup chopped onion

3 tablespoons butter or margarine

3 pounds beef chuck, cut into bite-size cubes

1 teaspoon caraway seeds

½ teaspoon marjoram

1 garlic clove, minced

1½ teaspoons salt

1½ cups water

2 tablespoons paprika

¼ cup ketchup

2 tablespoons water

1 pound green beans, cut

1 medium zucchini, sliced

1 green pepper, sliced

2 hard-boiled eggs, sliced

Paprika

1. In large saucepan or Dutch oven sauté onion in butter or margarine.

2. Add beef, caraway, marjoram, garlic, salt and 1½ cups water. Bring to a boil.

3. Make a paste of paprika, ketchup and the 2 tablespoons water; add to the meat mixture and blend in well.

4. Cover and simmer 1 hour.

5. If fresh green beans are used, add them and simmer, covered, for 5 minutes.

6. If green beans are frozen, add them with zucchini and green pepper; cover and simmer 10 minutes more.

7. Arrange egg slices on top of goulash, cover and simmer 5 minutes.

8. Sprinkle egg slices with paprika.

Serve with French or Italian bread.

Jean E. Thomson
William A. Thomson Jr. '46 C&F, '47 MA Econ

Nittany Stew

PREPARATION TIME: *4 hours*
YIELD: *6 – 8 servings*

1½ **pounds beef chuck, cut in cubes**

3 **cups sliced onion rings**

3 **cups sliced carrots**

2 **(10¾ ounce) cans cream of tomato soup**

2 **generous tablespoons sherry; do not use cooking sherry**

1. Spread half of the beef cubes on bottom of a 3-quart casserole. (Meat does not need to be browned.)

2. Cover with half of the onions.

3. Cover onions with half of the carrots. Repeat layering of beef, onions, and carrots.

4. Mix undiluted soup with sherry. Pour over beef, onions and carrots.

5. Cover and bake at 300° for 2½ hours. Remove lid and bake an additional 45 minutes.

Serve with wild rice. Great reheated, too!

Mary O'Connor Pfahl '40 HEc

Surprising Roasted Turkey Breast

PREPARATION TIME: *10 minutes plus marinating time, plus 1 hour 30 minutes baking time*

YIELD: *5 – 7 servings*

5 – 7 **pound fresh or frozen turkey breast, or one 3-pound boneless turkey breast**	1. Clean inside of fresh or defrosted turkey breast.
1 **medium onion, halved**	2. Rub inside and outside of breast with cut onion; reserve onion halves.
¼ **teaspoon onion powder**	3. Mix together onion powder, lemon pepper, garlic powder, poultry seasoning and ginger powder. Season turkey breast well.
¼ **teaspoon lemon pepper**	
¼ **teaspoon garlic powder**	
¼ **teaspoon poultry seasoning**	
¼ **teaspoon ginger powder**	4. Chop the halves of onion, celery and carrot and place under breast in pan (preferably a glass pan). Wrap with plastic wrap and refrigerate overnight or rest of day.
1 **carrot, chopped coarsely**	
1 **celery stalk, chopped coarsely**	
Vegetable spray for pan	5. Next day spray roaster or disposable aluminum pan with vegetable spray. Remove turkey from refrigerator, place in pan and let reach room temperature.
1 – 2 **cups ginger ale**	
Paprika	
¼ **teaspoon salt and 1 tablespoon margarine for top of breast (optional)**	6. Pour ginger ale over turkey breast.
	7. Sprinkle profusely with paprika.
	8. Preheat oven to 500° . Oven must be fully preheated.
	9. Bake, uncovered, for only 20 minutes. Do not peek in oven! For a very large breast, leave in 25 minutes. After initial time, turn oven off and leave turkey in oven without opening it for one hour and 10 minutes.

"If breast is too pink, it can be put back in 350 degree oven for a few more minutes, but this has seldom happened. I omit salt and margarine and this favorite dish is also a low-calorie and healthy one. You will be surprised the turkey is so moist and delicious. It can be served either hot or cold."

Judith Auritt Klein '47 Psy
Robert Klein '48 C&F

Fiesta Balls

PREPARATION TIME: *45 minutes*
YIELD: *4 servings*

1 **pound ground turkey**	1. Mix together turkey, bread crumbs, salt, and pepper.
¾ **cup bread crumbs**	
⅛ **teaspoon salt**	2. Stir in milk, egg, onion, sugar, nutmeg and allspice. Add enough oatmeal to absorb moisture. Shape into 1½"balls.
½ **teaspoon pepper**	

1. Mix together turkey, bread crumbs, salt, and pepper.

2. Stir in milk, egg, onion, sugar, nutmeg and allspice. Add enough oatmeal to absorb moisture. Shape into 1½"balls.

1 **pound ground turkey**

¾ **cup bread crumbs**

⅛ **teaspoon salt**

½ **teaspoon pepper**

½ **cup milk**

1 **egg**

1 **small onion, diced**

1 **tablespoon sugar**

¼ **teaspoon nutmeg**

⅛ **teaspoon allspice**

Oatmeal, enough to absorb moisture

¼ **cup butter**

2 **cups beef or chicken broth (or bouillon)**

2 **tablespoons chopped parsley**

3. In a flameproof casserole, melt butter. Brown the meatballs. Remove from heat and add the broth.

4. Cover and bake at 375° for 30 minutes, basting occasionally.

5. Sprinkle with parsley before serving.

Marci Jo Mongeau '87 HEEd

Check the type of "ground turkey." Commercial packages are allowed 29% fat by weight. Grind your own in a food processor or ask a butcher to process a turkey breast for you.

Nittany Chicken Curry

PREPARATION TIME: *1 hour 15 minutes*
YIELD: *6 – 8 servings*

1 medium onion, chopped

½ cup finely chopped celery

¼ cup butter

2 tablespoons cornstarch

2 cups chicken broth

1 whole chicken, cooked and meat removed from bones, cut into small pieces

1 teaspoon curry

4 cups hot cooked rice

1. Lightly brown onion and celery in butter. Add cornstarch and blend.

2. Add broth; cook until thick, stir constantly. If too thick, add additional chicken broth.

3. Add cooked chicken and curry powder, simmer to blend flavors (about 15 minutes).

4. Serve over cooked rice.

Michelle Klemo Tyson '77 RcPk

Brown rice contains more nutrients than white rice. Leftover rice can be stored in the refrigerator or freezer and reheated in a steamer basket easily.

Grilled Chicken Tailgaters' Delight

PREPARATION TIME: *45 minutes plus 1 day marinating time*
YIELD: *45 – 50 servings*

1 pint soy sauce

2½ cups cooking sherry

1 cup vinegar

3½ pints pineapple juice

1½ cups sugar

2½ teaspoons garlic powder

50 pieces boned chicken breast

1 can pineapple rings

1. Combine soy sauce, sherry, vinegar, pineapple juice, sugar and garlic powder. Marinate chicken for 24 hours.

2. Cook chicken with pineapple rings on charcoal grill. Brush marinade over chicken while cooking.

Janet L. Palamone '82 HPA

Roarin' Good Chicken

PREPARATION TIME: *1 hour 30 minutes*
YIELD: *6 – 8 servings*

8 chicken breasts, split and skinned

Ground pepper (optional)

Paprika (optional)

6 tablespoons unsalted butter

1 pound mushrooms, sliced

2 tablespoons flour

⅔ cup chicken broth

½ cup sherry

2 (6 ounce) jars marinated artichoke hearts, drained

1. Season chicken with pepper and paprika. Brown chicken in butter for 12 – 15 minutes. Remove chicken to baking dish.

2. Add mushrooms to skillet and sauté 5 minutes.

3. Stir in flour, broth, and sherry; cook 5 minutes.

4. Arrange artichokes over chicken. Pour sauce over chicken.

5. Bake, uncovered, at 375° for 1 hour.

Joanne Wagner Haskell '51 HEc

Creamy Baked Chicken Breasts

PREPARATION TIME: *1 hour*
YIELD: *5 – 8 servings*

4 whole chicken breasts, split, skinned and boned

8 slices Swiss cheese

1 (10¾ ounce) can cream of chicken soup

¼ cup dry white wine

1 cup herb-seasoned stuffing mix, crushed

¼ cup butter or margarine, melted

1. Arrange chicken in a lightly greased 9 × 13-inch baking dish. Top with cheese slices.

2. Combine soup and wine, stir well. Spoon sauce evenly over chicken, and sprinkle with stuffing mix.

3. Drizzle butter or margarine over crumbs.

4. Bake at 350° for 45 – 55 minutes.

Karen Nelson Carey '63 Psy

Chicken with Curry and Honey

PREPARATION TIME: *1 hour 15 minutes*
YIELD: *6 servings*

3 tablespoons milk

3 tablespoons melted butter

¼ cup prepared mustard

½ cup honey

1 teaspoon curry powder

1 teaspoon salt

3 pounds chicken parts

1. Mix milk, butter, mustard, honey, curry and salt together.

2. Dip chicken pieces in mixture and place pieces on a baking sheet or roasting pan.

3. Bake at 350° for 1 hour. Baste occasionally with remaining sauce.

LCdr. Janet T. Markle, MD '76 Biol, '78 MS Phys

Chicken Nittany

PREPARATION TIME: *45 minutes plus 2 hours marinating time*
YIELD: *4 – 6 servings*

3 **pounds boneless chicken breasts**	1. Pound chicken breasts a few times with a meat mallet to flatten slightly. Marinate in sherry or squeeze lemon juice on the chicken. Let set for 1 – 2 hours.
1 **cup lemon juice or sherry**	
1 **egg**	
¼ **cup milk**	2. Beat egg and milk together. Add thyme, marjoram, garlic powder, seasoned salt and pepper to egg mixture.
⅛ **teaspoon thyme**	
⅛ **teaspoon marjoram**	3. Dip breasts in egg mixture and coat in bread crumbs.
⅛ **teaspoon garlic powder**	
Seasoned salt, to taste	4. Heat oil and butter in large skillet. Cook chicken on both sides until tender and golden brown.
Black pepper, to taste	
1½ **cups seasoned bread crumbs**	5. Prepare mushroom sauce and pour over chicken to serve.
⅓ – ½ **cup olive oil**	
¼ **cup butter**	

MUSHROOM SAUCE

2 **tablespoons butter or margarine**	1. Melt butter or margarine in skillet over low heat.
1 **cup mushrooms, washed and sliced**	2. Add mushrooms and brown slowly before adding flour. Blend flour in, stir until flour is deep brown.
2 **tablespoons flour**	
1 **cup beef broth**	3. Remove from heat and stir in beef broth. Heat to boiling, stir constantly. Boil for 1 minute.
¼ **teaspoon salt**	
⅛ **teaspoon pepper**	4. Add salt and pepper; stir. Serve over chicken breasts.

Deborah Suggars Costantino '76 Nurs

Chicken Cordon Bleu and White

PREPARATION TIME: *1 hour*

YIELD: *4 servings*

4 ounces cream cheese, softened

6 ounces shredded Swiss cheese

2 cloves fresh garlic, minced

1 teaspoon freeze-dried chives

1 teaspoon fresh chopped parsley

4 slices baked ham

4 whole boneless chicken breasts

¼ cup butter

2 ounces bread crumbs

Paprika, to taste

1. Combine cream cheese, Swiss cheese, garlic, chives and parsley. Shape cheese mixture into 4 oblong logs, refrigerate until firm.

2. Place cheese logs on ham slices and fold slices up, tucking ends in.

3. Place log, seam side down, on breast of chicken (you may pound breast thin with a mallet). Shape breast around ham and place seam side down on ungreased baking sheet.

4. Lightly butter outside of breast to keep from drying out.

5. Sprinkle each breast with bread crumbs and paprika.

6. Bake at 325° for 30 – 40 minutes.

7. Serve with rice or rice pilaf.

Constance E. Butler '82 FSHA

Chicken Enchiladas

PREPARATION TIME: *2 hours*

YIELD: *4 – 6 servings*

2 whole chicken breasts

½ small onion

1 bay leaf

8 peppercorns

Salt (optional)

Water to cover

½ medium onion, diced

3 tablespoons grated Parmesan cheese

4 ounces Monterey Jack cheese, shredded

1 (4 ounce) can green chilies

1 (13 ounce) can tomatillos, drained or 1 pound fresh

1 teaspoon coriander, ground

2 teaspoons cilantro, ground or ⅛ cup fresh

¾ cup whipping cream

1 egg

¼ cup lard or shortening

12 corn tortillas

4 ounces Cheddar cheese, shredded

Sour cream

Salsa

1. Combine first 6 ingredients in a large pot. Bring to boil, then reduce heat and simmer 45 minutes. Cool chicken in broth, drain. Shred chicken with two forks or your fingers or grind in meat grinder.

2. Mix shredded chicken with onion, Parmesan and Monterey Jack cheeses. Set aside.

3. In blender or food processor, combine the chilies, tomatillos, coriander, cilantro, whipping cream and egg. Blend until smooth and set aside.

4. Heat lard in a small skillet. With tongs, carefully place one tortilla at a time in hot lard and hold there, turning if necessary, 10 – 20 seconds until softened; drain over skillet or on paper towels.

5. Place 1/12th of the chicken mixture on each tortilla, pressing the mixture to make it compact. Roll tightly and place seam side down in a 8 × 12-inch baking dish. Pour tomatillo mixture over enchiladas and sprinkle evenly with Cheddar or Monterey Jack cheese.

6. Bake at 350° for 20 minutes.

7. To serve top with sour cream and salsa.

If fresh tomatillos are used, remove papery husks, wash and simmer in saucepan for 10 minutes. Drain. The first 3 steps can be done ahead of time and frozen.

Sally White Wackowski '80 IE
Ronald K. Wackowski '80 PNGE

Warm tortillas by wrapping in foil and heating in oven, rather than frying.

Enchilada Chicken

PREPARATION TIME: *30 minutes*
YIELD: *2 servings*

½ **cup cooked chopped broccoli**

½ **cup plain lowfat yogurt**

Garlic powder, to taste

¼ **teaspoon lemon juice**

6 **ounces cooked chicken, skinned and diced**

4 **six-inch flour tortillas**

3 **ounces grated Cheddar cheese**

1. Combine broccoli, yogurt, garlic powder and lemon juice in a small bowl; mix well.

2. Place one half of mixture in another bowl and add chicken.

3. Heat a nonstick skillet and warm tortillas for 15 seconds on each side.

4. Place one-fourth of the chicken mixture on each tortilla. Roll tortillas up and place seam-side down in a small baking dish.

5. Top the enchiladas with the remaining broccoli-yogurt mixture.

6. Cover with cheese and bake at 350° for 15 minutes or until the cheese melts.

Kathryn A. Petrich-LaFevre '82 Engl

Many of us can remember having to remain on campus at least one holiday during our stay at PSU. One alumna tells of her Thanksgiving experience:

During my senior year, I couldn't go home for Thanksgiving with our family because I had an exam on Friday morning after Turkey Day. My father, who is a chef, felt badly that I was missing our traditional Thanksgiving feast. So his solution was to send me a complete Thanksgiving feast (fully prepared, ready to be warmed up and served) via Greyhound Bus. A friend and his friend and several sorority sisters dined on turkey, sweet potatoes, mashed potatoes, pumpkin pie, cranberries, bread, rolls and apple pie. A most memorable Thanksgiving Feast.

Szechwan Chicken Stir-Fry

PREPARATION TIME: *1 hour*
YIELD: *6 servings*

MARINADE

- 1 tablespoon soy sauce
- 1 tablespoon sherry wine
- 1 tablespoon sugar
- 1 tablespoon water
- 1 teaspoon minced garlic
- ½ teaspoon fresh ground black pepper

- 2½ pounds boneless chicken breasts, cut in strips

1. Mix marinade ingredients together.
2. Add chicken and marinate for 15 minutes.

SAUCE

- 3 cups water
- 2 teaspoons sugar
- 6 tablespoons soy sauce
- 2 tablespoons sherry wine
- 3½ tablespoons cornstarch
- 1 teaspoon dried red pepper
- ¼ teaspoon thyme
- ½ teaspoon basil
- ⅛ teaspoon rosemary

1. Mix sauce ingredients together to dissolve cornstarch; set aside to add later.

VEGETABLES

- 6 tablespoons olive oil
- 3½ cups broccoli cut in small pieces
- 2 green peppers, cut in strips
- 2 onions, cut in slices
- 2 carrots, cut diagonally

- 1 pound mushrooms, sliced

1. Heat 3 tablespoons oil in wok and saute chicken mixture until opaque. Remove chicken and set aside.
2. Heat 3 tablespoons oil in wok and add broccoli, peppers, onions and carrots stir-frying until crunchy, about 5 – 8 minutes.
3. Add mushrooms and cook 1 minute.
4. Add chicken and sauce mixture to vegetables. Bring to a boil and simmer 2 – 3 minutes.
5. Adjust seasonings with salt and pepper. Serve over boiled rice.

Donald A. Remley '82 2MET

Lafayette-Style Creole Chicken

PREPARATION TIME: *20 minutes plus 1 hour cooking time*
YIELD: *4 servings*

4 tablespoons margarine

1 large onion, finely chopped

1 large green pepper, chopped

2 stalks celery, chopped

1 teaspoon cayenne pepper

1 teaspoon salt

1 teaspoon thyme

½ teaspoon black pepper

½ teaspoon sage

4 chicken breasts, skinned

2 carrots, sliced

1 (28 ounce) can tomatoes

1 (8 ounce) can tomato sauce

1 (10¾ ounce) can cream of chicken soup

2 teaspoons sugar

2 whole bay leaves

2 cups Burgundy wine

1. Melt margarine in large pot over medium heat.

2. Sauté onion, green pepper and celery for about 10 minutes.

3. Add cayenne pepper, salt, thyme, black pepper, and sage, cooking for another 2 minutes.

4. Add chicken and remaining ingredients.

5. Cover and simmer until chicken is tender, about 1 hour.

6. Serve over rice.

Ronald Q. Warren '76 Biol

Big Apple Coq Au Vin

PREPARATION TIME: *1 hour 20 minutes*

YIELD: *6 servings*

CASSEROLE

2½ – 3 pounds chicken pieces

    Breading mixture (recipe below)

4 tablespoons vegetable shortening

4 slices bacon, cut into 1 inch pieces

¼ teaspoon garlic powder

2 tablespoons parsley

1 teaspoon dried onion soup mix

1 bay leaf

1 tablespoon breading mixture

1 cup water or 1 cup canned onion soup

1 cup red wine

1 (8 ounce) can onions, drained

1 (3 ounce) can mushrooms, drained

1. Wash chicken and dry off excess moisture. Coat chicken pieces with breading mixture.

2. In an electric skillet set at 350° brown chicken in small amount of fat for about 15 minutes.

3. Add bacon pieces and brown.

4. Add garlic powder, parsley, onion soup mix, bay leaf and reserved breading mixture.

5. Add water or canned onion soup and wine; set electric fry pan to simmer; simmer about 30 minutes.

6. Add onions and mushrooms and cook for 10 minutes.

BREADING MIXTURE

½ cup all-purpose flour

1 teaspoon salt

¼ teaspoon pepper

2 tablespoons dry onion soup mix

1. Combine all ingredients together.

Natalie Dabich Bailey '69 IFS
Michael S. Bailey '64 BA

Chicken Mornay

PREPARATION TIME: *1 hour 15 minutes*
YIELD: *4 servings*

1 **(10 ounce) package frozen broccoli spears**	1. Cook broccoli until barely tender and drain.
¼ **cup butter or margarine**	2. Arrange broccoli in buttered 1½-quart casserole.
¼ **cup all-purpose flour**	
1 **cup poultry broth**	3. In separate saucepan, melt butter or margarine and stir in flour.
½ **cup heavy cream**	
½ **cup dry white wine**	4. Add broth and cream. Cook until sauce is thick and smooth, stirring constantly.
Salt and pepper, to taste	
⅛ **teaspoon Worcestershire sauce**	5. Stir in wine, salt and pepper to taste, and Worcestershire sauce.
2 **cups chopped cooked chicken**	6. Top broccoli with chicken, mushrooms, and water chestnuts (if desired).
1 **(4 ounce) can sliced mushrooms**	
⅓ **(8 ounce) can water chestnuts, thinly sliced (optional)**	7. Cover with sauce and sprinkle with cheese.
⅓ **cup grated Parmesan cheese**	8. Bake, uncovered, at 425° for 15 – 20 minutes.

Jane E. Nichols '66 Engl

To make a low-fat roux, mix ¼ cup flour, 1 cup defatted poultry broth and ½ cup skim milk in a shaker or jar. Omit butter. Heat in saucepan until thick and creamy.

Indonesian Chicken

PREPARATION TIME: *1 hour plus marinating time*
YIELD: *8 servings*

½ **cup minced onion**

2 **cloves garlic, minced**

½ **teaspoon dried ground chili pepper**

½ **cup peanut butter**

1 **teaspoon salt**

2 **teaspoons salad oil**

2 **tablespoons soy sauce**

1 **cup water**

2 **tablespoons lime or lemon juice**

2 **(total 3 pounds) broilers or fryer chickens, cut into quarters**

1. Combine onion, garlic, chili pepper, peanut butter and salt. Sauté in oil for 3 minutes.

2. Add soy sauce, water, lime or lemon juice and cook over low heat about 5 minutes.

3. Remove from heat; cool.

4. Marinate chicken pieces in sauce at least 1 hour, then broil 25 – 30 minutes, turning the chicken several times. Baste frequently with marinade.

5. Heat remaining marinade and serve as a sauce with chicken.

Thomas M. Dabich '73 Journ

Penn State's food service serves 6 million meals a year.

Far East Chicken

PREPARATION TIME: *10 minutes plus 50 minutes cooking time*
YIELD: *4 servings*

¾ **cup vermouth**

¼ **cup soy sauce or tamari**

¼ **cup salad oil**

1 **tablespoon brown sugar**

¼ **teaspoon oregano**

1 **teaspoon ginger**

2 **tablespoons water**

4 **boned chicken breasts**

1. Combine vermouth, soy sauce or tamari, salad oil, brown sugar, oregano, ginger and water in jar. Shake well to mix.

2. Place chicken in a flat baking dish and pour mixture over chicken.

3. Bake at 375° for 50 minutes turning once.

"Sam keeps the jar in the refrigerator, drains mixture after chicken is baked, and stores it for use over and over."

Helen Dobbins Casey
Samuel B. Casey Jr. '50 C&F

Skin chicken or turkey before cooking to eliminate calories.

Oriental Chicken Casserole

PREPARATION TIME: *45 minutes*
YIELD: *8 servings*

3 chicken breasts, cooked and diced

2 (10¾ ounce) cans cream of chicken soup, undiluted

1 (14 ounce) can chop suey vegetables

1 (8 ounce) can water chestnuts, drained and sliced

1 (5 ounce) can crisp Chinese noodles

1 cup chopped celery

½ cup mayonnaise

1 tablespoon lemon juice

2 tablespoons chopped onions

Cashew nuts

1. Combine all ingredients using only half the can of crisp noodles. Pour into a buttered 9 × 13-inch casserole dish.

2. Sprinkle remaining noodles on top, then add sliced cashews.

3. Bake uncovered at 350° for 30 minutes.

Catherine King Zernhelt '59 BA
Francis L. Zernhelt '61 BA

During the breakfast rush or after the downtown bars close, 25-30 stickies come out of the Diner's kitchen every minute.

Chicken Liver Sauté

PREPARATION TIME: *15 minutes*
YIELD: *2 servings*

8 ounces chicken livers

Seasoned flour (recipe below)

1 tablespoon bacon fat

1 cup mushrooms, cleaned and quartered

2 tablespoons sherry wine

4 scallions, sliced

1. Coat livers, one at a time, in seasoned flour, sauté in bacon fat over medium-low heat until browned. Turn each liver once, continue to cook for another 2 – 3 minutes.

2. Add mushrooms, remove from heat and add sherry wine, return to heat and sauté until wine has reduced and thickened lightly.

3. Add scallions, mix gently. Serve immediately.

SEASONED FLOUR

1 cup flour

1 tablespoon seasoned salt

1 teaspoon white pepper

1 teaspoon garlic salt

1. Combine all ingredients and mix well. Store in airtight container.

Richard A. Benefield '48 HA

Penn State Stir-Fry

PREPARATION TIME: *40 minutes*
YIELD: *4 – 6 servings*

1 teaspoon cornstarch

¼ teaspoon ground ginger

2 tablespoons soy sauce

2 tablespoons dry sherry

½ cup chicken broth

2 tablespoons salad oil

1 clove garlic, minced or pressed

½ pound shrimp, cut up

½ pound boneless chicken, cut up

1 cup snow peas, ends and strings removed

3 chive or onion stalks, cut up

1 cup bean sprouts

1. Mix cornstarch and ginger; then blend in soy sauce, sherry, broth and set aside.

2. Place wok over high heat. When wok is hot add oil. When oil is hot add garlic, shrimp and chicken. Stir fry for two minutes.

3. Add vegetables, stir fry for two minutes.

4. Add cornstarch mixture, blend well. Stir until contents come to a boil and sauce thickens.

5. Serve over rice.

Debra Przywara McRae '81 Micrb

To increase fiber and decrease calories, add additional vegetables to stir-frys. Replace part of the meat with tofu cubes marinated in low-sodium soy sauce.

Shrimply Delicious

PREPARATION TIME: *40 minutes plus chilling time*
YIELD: *5 – 7 servings*

2 pounds raw shrimp in the shell

1 lemon, thinly sliced

1 large red onion, thinly sliced

1 cup whole pitted ripe olives

2 tablespoons chopped pimiento

½ cup freshly squeezed lemon juice

¼ cup salad oil

1 tablespoon wine vinegar

1 clove garlic, minced

1 bay leaf, broken

1 tablespoon dry mustard

¼ teaspoon cayenne pepper

Freshly ground black pepper, to taste

1 teaspoon salt

1. Shell and devein the raw shrimp. Bring 4 quarts water to a boil and add the shrimp; cook for three minutes. Drain at once and combine the hot shrimp with lemon and onion slices, olives, and pimiento.

2. In a large bowl combine the lemon juice, oil, vinegar, and seasonings. Stir in the shrimp mixture; toss and mix well to thoroughly coat the shrimp. Cover and refrigerate overnight, stir once or twice. (Or you can store the mixture in a zipped plastic bag and turn it several times.)

3. To serve, spoon from the bowl onto small lettuce-lined plates for individual servings. For a group, serve in an attractive bowl (lettuce-lined if desired) with toothpicks for spearing.

Barbara Gomber Isham '61 SecEd

Halftime Shrimp

PREPARATION TIME: *20 minutes*

YIELD: *4 – 6 servings as an entree, 12 or more as an appetizer*

1½ **pounds medium unpeeled shrimp**

Olive oil

Black pepper

Salt

Lemon juice

Hot sauce or tabasco sauce

Worcestershire sauce

Butter

1. Place unpeeled shrimp in a single layer in the bottom part of a broiler pan.

2. Drizzle shrimp with olive oil. Pepper shrimp until they are black, then add more pepper. Sprinkle with salt. Add a lot of lemon juice, hot sauce and Worcestershire sauce.

3. Cut up butter (½ cup per pound of shrimp) and place on top of shrimp.

4. Broil until shrimp are cooked, about 10 – 15 minutes.

5. Serve with French bread for dipping, a green salad and a lot of beer.

"This is probably the most bizarre recipe that my wife and I have in our files. It's very easy and is perfect for preparing at half time of a televised Penn State game. You can start from scratch and still not miss anything but commercials.

If you use medium shrimp, you are supposed to eat everything, but I usually don't eat the tails. The "sauce" softens up the shells, they are delicious! Don't be intimidated by the ingredients. I have made this dish for probably a hundred people and everyone loves it."

Joan Lentz Knepper '70 EKEd
William D. Knepper '70 QBA

Crevettes à la Lion (Shrimp)

PREPARATION TIME: *45 minutes*
YIELD: *6 servings*

2 tablespoons butter	1. Melt butter in saucepan.
¾ cup finely chopped carrots	2. Add carrots, onions, celery, garlic and tomato. Cook over low heat for 5 – 10 minutes.
½ cup finely chopped onions	
½ cup finely chopped green onions	3. Add shrimp and continue cooking until vegetables are limp and shrimp are pink.
½ cup finely chopped celery	
2 garlic cloves, finely chopped	4. Add Veloute sauce, pepper and parsley and cook without boiling for 10 more minutes.
1 medium tomato, finely chopped	
2 cups small peeled shrimp	5. To serve, spoon mixture into 6 individual ovenproof dishes. Mix grated cheeses and bread crumbs together and sprinkle over the top.
1½ cups Veloute sauce (recipe below)	
Dash of white pepper	6. Bake at 400° for about 25 minutes or until the cheese melts and the top begins to brown.
1 tablespoon chopped parsley	
3 tablespoons grated Swiss cheese	
3 tablespoons grated Romano cheese	
3 tablespoons grated mozzarella cheese	
¼ cup seasoned bread crumbs	

VELOUTE SAUCE

2 tablespoons butter	1. Melt butter and stir in flour. Stir and cook until mixture becomes foamy.
2 tablespoons flour	
1½ cups chicken broth	2. Add chicken broth and bring to a boil, stir constantly. Reduce heat and simmer until thick.

"The time consuming part of the recipe is the chopping of vegetables and grating of cheeses. A food processor is ideal."

Martha (Marty) Whipple Gasche

Shrimp Packages From The Grill

PREPARATION TIME: *20 minutes*
YIELD: *4 servings*

1 **pound jumbo shrimp, peeled and deveined**

4 **scallions, sliced**

2 **small zucchini, sliced**

4 **large mushrooms, sliced**

Juice of 1 lemon

Marjoram

1 **garlic clove, minced (optional)**

1. Cut and grease four 12 × 12-inch pieces of heavy duty aluminum foil.

2. Place equal amounts of shrimp, scallions, zucchini and mushrooms on each piece of foil.

3. Sprinkle with lemon juice, marjoram and garlic.

4. Double fold edges of foil, sealing well.

5. Place shrimp on hot grill and cook about 10 minutes or until done.

Nancy M. O'Connor

Grilled Swordfish

PREPARATION TIME: *15 minutes plus 2 – 4 hours marinating time*
YIELD: *4 – 6 servings*

1½ – 2 **pounds swordfish steaks**

¼ **teaspoon pepper**

½ **teaspoon dill**

1 **teaspoon dry or fresh chopped parsley**

½ **teaspoon dry oregano**

¼ – ½ **cup teriyaki sauce**

2 **tablespoons soy sauce**

1. Wash fish steaks and pat dry. Place in shallow baking dish.

2. Mix the remaining ingredients and pour over fish.

3. Turn fish and marinate 2 – 4 hours in refrigerator, turning once again.

4. Oil grill slightly.

5. Cook on medium fire 6 – 8 minutes on each side, depending on thickness of steaks. Serve immediately.

Margaret A. Kuss '81 Acctg

Low-sodium soy sauce makes this marinade healthier.

Walleye Encasserole

PREPARATION TIME: *40 minutes*
YIELD: *6 servings*

1 **cup sour cream**

½ **cup white wine**

1 **tablespoon flour**

½ **cup chopped mild onion**

Salt and pepper, to taste

2 **pounds walleye or other fish fillets**

Paprika (optional)

1. Mix sour cream, wine, flour, onion, salt and pepper together.

2. Place fillets in 9 × 12-inch greased baking dish.

3. Pour sour cream mixture over fillets.

4. Sprinkle with paprika if desired.

5. Bake at 350° for 30 minutes.

Patricia B. Beam
Robert E. Beam '48 C&F

Try this healthy fish recipe with ½ cup sour cream and ½ cup plain non-fat yogurt.

Butterflied Leg of Lamb

PREPARATION TIME: *45 minutes plus 1 hour marinating time*
YIELD: *6 servings*

1 **6 – 7 pound leg of lamb, boned and butterflied**

1 **clove garlic, crushed**

¾ **cup salad oil**

¼ **cup red wine vinegar**

½ **cup chopped onion**

2 **teaspoons Dijon mustard**

2 **teaspoons salt**

½ **teaspoon oregano**

½ **teaspoon basil**

⅛ **teaspoon freshly ground black pepper**

1 **bay leaf, crushed**

1. Place lamb fat side down in shallow pan.

2. In a small bowl mix the garlic, oil, vinegar, onion, mustard, salt, oregano, basil, pepper and bay leaf to form a marinade.

3. Pour marinade mixture over lamb. Cover pan tightly and refrigerate overnight, turning meat at least once.

4. Remove lamb from refrigerator at least 1 hour before cooking.

5. Place meat and marinade in broiler pan, fat side up and broil 4 inches from heat for 10 minutes.

6. Turn meat over, baste and broil 10 minutes on other side.

7. Reduce oven temperature to 425°, transfer meat to oven and roast meat for 15 minutes.

8. Test for doneness with sharp knife. Meat should be pink and juicy.

9. Carve meat into thin slices.

Sandra L. Rothwell

Flounder and Rice à la Cape May

PREPARATION TIME: *30 minutes plus 15 minutes cooking time*
YIELD: *4 servings*

¾ **cup rice**

2 **cups chicken broth**

½ **cup butter**

1 **pound flounder fillets**

⅓ **pound peeled and seeded or seedless green grapes**

1. Cook rice in chicken broth for 15 minutes. Place in bottom of 9 × 13-inch casserole.

2. Prepare cheese sauce.

3. Divide butter into 4 large or 8 small pieces. Cut flounder fillets to the same number.

4. Roll each fillet around a piece of butter. Place on top of rice.

5. Cover fish fillets with cheese sauce.

6. Sprinkle with grapes.

7. Bake at 350° for 15 minutes.

CHEESE SAUCE

3 **tablespoons butter**

3 **tablespoons flour**

1 **cup chicken broth**

½ **cup cream or evaporated milk**

⅔ **cup grated Cheddar cheese**

Salt and pepper, to taste

1. Melt butter in saucepan and blend in flour until smooth.

2. Add chicken broth and cream, cook until thick, stir constantly.

3. Add cheese and stir until melted.

4. Season with salt and pepper.

Mandarin oranges may be substituted for grapes.

Marybelle Crossman Harris '41 HEc

Themes

The use of themes is a primary planning tool of Penn State's Office of Special Events. Always, with an eye to budget and good taste, the staff works to achieve a friendly and unique ambience for each of the President's events at his home in Boalsburg, at University House and at other campus locations.

"Dinner in the Orient," given in honor of Palmer Museum of Art benefactors, featured an invitation presented in a fan shape — delicate Japanese rice paper unfolded to reveal calligraphy in black with red and gold accents. Oriental floral arrangements and food specialties created the appropriate exotic and elegant atmosphere for the event itself.

A theme dessert party for members of the University Student Executive Council was introduced with a rich brown invitation, the word "chocolate" splashed across the front in white crayon. A delectable array of chocolate desserts was served with — what else? — chocolate sodas.

For another student event, a "Super Sundae Tuesday" party was created featuring Penn State Creamery ice cream and a variety of soda-fountain toppings.

Penn State produce — fresh from the experimental farms — provided the idea for a "Really Raspberry Afternoon Tea." This event, for retired faculty women and outstanding women volunteers in the community, featured hot pink invitations with white lettering, raspberry scones, tarts and iced drinks, and tiny baskets of fresh berries given as a take-home favor to each guest.

Kites — a harbinger of spring — are festive, low-cost items to decorate your first spring party. In March they became the focal point for a University House reception. Inspired by childhood memories of kite-flying, the Special Events staff developed a theme of "Kiting in Central Park."

Carrying out the theme were lively wind socks flying from the balcony to greet guests as they approached University House. Delta kites hung from the reception room ceiling and floated above the entering guests. More wind socks, with their tails tucked in, were filled with plastic containers of colorful spring flowers, and these "vases" were surrounded by green "Easter-basket" grass. Bright grass-green table linen with white skirting and cocktail napkins in brilliant yellow, pink, green and blue completed the ensemble for a cheerful, breezy effect.

Food like the kinds you might purchase from a vendor while kiting in Central Park was the order of the day — shish kebabs, mini-bagels with a cream cheese and lox spread, mini-Reubens, mini-burritos, and cheese with fresh fruit. Sparkling New York Seltzers, served in their bottles with straws, were the featured beverage.

The day of the event was resplendent with bright sunshine and a beautiful blue sky. It was rewarding to hear the guests' delighted comments about their opportunity to enjoy kiting in the Central Park of Central Pennsylvania.

Football tailgating events provide opportunities for great fun — think of all the "pawsibilities!" Use the clever manipulation of "Lion wording" on invitations ("A purrfectly pawsta tailgate") and menu selections ("Penn State-ly Soup"). Try Lion decorations — cut-out paw prints leading from the front door to the buffet table, or use smaller ones for name tags.

A theme will get you going, keep you going in the right direction and let your guests know that you truly enjoyed planning the party for them. It will set the perfect tone for the delightful experience you and your guests will have — whatever the occasion!

Eggs and Dairy

The versatility of using ingredients several ways is one of the joys of cooking. Eggs, milk and cheese offer you the greatest variety — from hurry-up breakfasts to leisurely lunches, from snappy first courses to superlative desserts.

A repertoire of tried-and-true dishes from this section are an asset to any host and hostess and are invaluable to those of you who lead busy lives.

Keep in mind several bonuses! . . .

   . . . Universal appeal of dairy-based dishes
   . . . Ease of substituting to accommodate special diets without losing quality or taste
   . . . Simplicity of menu planning by adding an easy green salad or fresh fruit to a main-course dairy dish
   . . . Prepare-ahead value of many of these recipes

Try the Crusty Creamery Cheese Memories as an occasional substitute for pizza; Old Main Omelet for an anniversary breakfast; Lion Lover's Lasagna for your family reunion; Reuben Quiche for the men's next card game; and the Cornmeal Eggs as a change from the usual!

For quick treats, remember the instant success of presenting a few wedges of beautiful cheese in their natural state or serving a giant scoop of delicious ice cream. Don't forget the refreshing taste of cold milk all by itself or with fresh-baked morsels! Fortunate are those who leave the Creamery with a well-stocked cooler!

Cheesy Zucchini Pie

PREPARATION TIME: *40 minutes*
YIELD: *8 – 10 servings*

1 cup Bisquick	1. Mix all ingredients together.
½ cup finely chopped onion	2. Spread in a greased 9 × 13-inch pan.
½ cup grated cheese, Parmesan or Romano	3. Bake at 350° for 25 minutes or until golden brown.
2 tablespoons snipped parsley	
½ teaspoon salt	
½ teaspoon seasoned salt	
½ teaspoon dried marjoram or oregano	
Dash pepper	
½ teaspoon garlic powder	
½ cup salad oil	
4 eggs, slightly beaten	
3 cups thinly sliced zucchini	

Cheryl Polizzi Barrett '80 MEd AEd

Biscuit mix and the cheeses already have salt. Omit the salt and seasoned salt. If the zucchini are young and tender, slice with the skins on for more vitamins and fiber.

Sackin' Seafood Quiche

PREPARATION TIME: *15 minutes plus 45 minutes cooking time*
YIELD: *6 servings*

4 **eggs, slightly beaten**

¾ **cup half and half**

1 **(4 ounce) can mushroom pieces or slices**

1 **9-inch pre-baked pie crust**

8 **ounces Swiss cheese, sliced**

1 **pound seafood sea legs, crumbled**

Salt and pepper, to taste

1. Mix slightly beaten eggs together with half and half.

2. Add the mushrooms, and set aside.

3. Line the pie crust with Swiss cheese slices.

4. Scatter crumbled sea legs over the cheese.

5. Pour the egg mixture over entire cheese and seafood mixture.

6. Bake at 375° for 45 – 50 minutes.

Can be frozen.

Tammy Carrara
Kris S. Carrara '83 CE

Fresh mushrooms can be steamed and added in place of canned ones.

Reuben Quiche

PREPARATION TIME: *20 minutes plus 40 minutes baking time*
YIELD: *4 – 6 servings*

1 **9-inch unbaked pastry crust**	1. Sprinkle seeds over pie crust, prick bottom of crust and bake at 375° for 7 minutes.
1 **tablespoon caraway seeds**	
8 **ounces corned beef, shredded**	2. Fill bottom of shell with corned beef and spread mustard over meat.
1½ **tablespoons Dijon mustard**	
¾ **cup sauerkraut, drained and squeezed**	3. Top with sauerkraut and then Swiss cheese. (Can be done ahead to this point.)
2 **cups grated Swiss cheese**	
2 **eggs, beaten**	4. Mix eggs, cream or half and half, onion, dry mustard and salt; pour over meat and cheese. (You can also pre-mix the eggs, cream and seasonings, then pour over meat and cheese just before baking.)
1 **cup light cream or half and half**	
1 **tablespoon grated onion**	
½ **teaspoon dry mustard**	
½ **teaspoon salt**	5. Bake at 375° for 40 minutes.
	6. Let stand for 5 minutes before slicing.

Nancy Bollenbacher Morrow '60

Omitting salt in an "already salty" recipe is wise. In this one, the corned beef, mustard, sauerkraut and cheese all contain salt.

178

Mushroom Crust Quiche

PREPARATION TIME: *15 minutes plus 30 minutes baking time*
YIELD: *6 servings*

¾ **pound mushrooms, coarsely chopped**

5 **tablespoons butter**

½ **cup finely crushed saltines**

¾ **cup sliced green or spring onions with tops**

8 **ounces Monterey Jack cheese, shredded**

1 **cup cottage cheese**

3 **eggs**

¼ **teaspoon pepper**

¼ **teaspoon paprika**

1. Sauté mushrooms in 3 tablespoons butter until limp.

2. Add saltine crumbs and mix well. Spread into buttered 9-inch pie pan.

3. Sauté onions in remaining 2 tablespoons butter for one minute. Spread onions over mushroom crust.

4. Sprinkle shredded cheese over onions.

5. Blend together the cottage cheese, eggs and pepper until smooth. Carefully pour mixture over other ingredients in pie pan.

6. Garnish with paprika.

7. Bake at 350° for 30 minutes or until knife inserted comes out clean.

Patrice L. Melcher '81 PNGE

Unsalted whole grain crackers would increase the fiber. The first ingredient on the cracker label should read "whole wheat flour". "Wheat flour" means it's white flour.

Speedy Spinach Pie

PREPARATION TIME: *1 hour*

YIELD: *20 servings on a buffet*

3 eggs	1. In medium bowl beat eggs.
2 cups milk	2. Mix in milk, flour, baking powder, salt, spinach and half of the melted margarine
2 cups flour	
2 teaspoons baking powder	3. Pour into a greased 9 × 13-inch pan.
½ teaspoon salt	4. Top with feta cheese.
1 (10 ounce) package frozen chopped spinach, defrosted and well drained	5. Drizzle remaining margarine over top.
¾ cup margarine, melted	6. Bake at 350° for 40 – 50 minutes or until lightly browned on top.
8 ounces feta cheese, sliced or crumbled	

Lucille Kreisman Safferman '54 Ed

To keep arteries healthier, make recipe with 1 egg and 4 egg whites, skim milk, no salt, and omit the margarine drizzled on top. The feta cheese has enough fat.

Crustless Spinach Quiche

PREPARATION TIME: *1 hour 15 minutes*
YIELD: *6 servings*

1 tablespoon salad or olive oil	1. Heat oil in skillet. Sauté onion until wilted.
1 large onion, chopped	
1 (10 ounce) package frozen chopped spinach, thawed and drained	2. Add spinach, cook until excess moisture is evaporated. Let cool.
5 eggs	3. Beat eggs in bowl. Add cheese and cinnamon. Season to taste with salt and pepper.
12 ounces Muenster cheese, shredded	4. Combine spinach and egg mixtures and turn into a greased 9-inch pie pan.
⅛ teaspoon cinnamon	5. Bake at 350° until nicely browned, 40 – 45 minutes.
Salt and pepper, to taste	

JoAnn Koch Shore '73 IFS, '75 MEd CnEd

Do you remember an old Home Ec "first" for freshmen in Food Prep 101 in the 1930s, Eggs à la Goldenrod?

Chili Rellenos

PREPARATION TIME: *30 minutes plus chilling time and 45 minutes baking time*
YIELD: *6 – 8 servings*

1 **(14 ounce) can green chilies**

1¼ **pounds Monterey Jack cheese, coarsely grated**

10 **eggs**

½ **pint heavy cream (or evaporated milk)**

1. Butter a 9 × 13-inch glass dish and make three alternating layers of chilies and cheese, starting with cheese.

2. Refrigerate until an hour before ready to serve.

3. One hour before serving, whip eggs; add heavy cream and mix well.

4. Pour over chilies and cheese.

5. Bake at 300° for 45 minutes.

Broccoli can be used instead of chilies.

Jackie Holland

Evaporated skim milk works great in recipes like this.

Overnight Wine and Cheese Omelet

PREPARATION TIME: *45 minutes plus overnight chilling and 70 minutes cooking time*

YIELD: *12 – 16 servings*

1	loaf day-old Italian bread cut into 1-inch cubes
6	tablespoons unsalted butter, melted
¾	pound Swiss cheese, grated
½	pound Monterey Jack cheese, grated
4	large scallions or green onions
16	eggs
3¼	cups milk
⅓	cup dry white wine
1	tablespoon Dijon mustard
¼	teaspoon freshly ground pepper
⅛	teaspoon cayenne pepper
½	pound thinly sliced prosciutto (or 1 pound cooked bacon or ¾ pound cooked sausage drained and crumbled)
1½	cups sour cream
⅔ – 1	cup Asiago or Parmesan cheese, grated

1. Butter two 9 × 13-inch baking dishes. Divide bread cubes evenly in both.

2. Drizzle melted butter evenly over bread cubes in each dish.

3. Shred Swiss and Monterey Jack cheese using grating disc in food processor and spread evenly over buttered bread cubes.

4. In food processor using blade knife, coarsely chop scallions; leave in processor.

5. In same bowl process half of the eggs, half of the milk, wine, mustard, and seasonings. Process until foamy. Pour into large pitcher. Repeat with remaining ingredients. Mix both batches together.

6. Pour evenly over cheese.

7. Layer prosciutto over egg mixture. Cover with heavy duty foil, crimping edges. Refrigerate overnight or up to 24 hours.

8. Remove from refrigerator 30 minutes before baking.

9. Bake at 325° for 1 hour or until set.

10. Uncover, spread with sour cream and sprinkle with Asiago or Parmesan cheese.

11. Return to oven and bake uncovered until crusty and lightly browned, about 10 minutes.

This is a traditional New Year's Day dish so none of the bowl games are missed.

Sandra Sabol MacDonald '69 MedT

Think about substituting low fat dairy products. Include vegetables and fruits in the menu to provide balanced nutrition.

Old Main Omelet

PREPARATION TIME: *20 – 25 minutes*
YIELD: *2 servings*

1	**apple (your favorite)**
3	**sausage patties or links**
1	**slice wheat bread**
3	**tablespoons butter, divided**
1	**teaspoon chopped pecans**
3 or 4	**eggs**
1	**tablespoon light cream**
3	**slices cheese**

1. Peel apple and slice into ¼" slices.

2. Place sausage into hot frying pan; after several minutes use wooden spatula to cut into small chunks.

3. Trim crust from bread and cut into croutons. Toast croutons in 1 tablespoon butter in separate frying pan, turning to brown all sides.

4. When sausage is slightly crispy, place on paper towel to drain excess fat.

5. Put apple slices in sausage drippings and sauté; when almost done, add chopped pecans.

6. Combine sausage, apples, pecans and croutons in small bowl for later use.

7. Beat eggs and cream until mixture is foamy.

8. Place remaining 2 tablespoons of butter into clean, very hot frying pan; shift pan so that entire surface of pan is coated with butter; make sure that pan is hot.

9. Add egg and cream mixture before butter has a chance to burn.

10. Immediately after adding egg mixture, shake pan to prevent omelet from sticking to surface; continue to shift pan to distribute liquid and allow it to run to bottom of pan.

11. With a slight amount of liquid remaining, pour the bowl of previously cooked sausage, apples, croutons and pecans onto half of the omelet and top off with the 3 slices of cheese.

12. Fold the other half over by tipping pan and using wooden spatula to help close the omelet.

13. Cut omelet in half while still in pan and slide each half onto warm plates; serve with warm muffins or toast and preserves.

Gerald L. Hess '66 Acctg

Penn State "Bleu" Cheese Omelet

PREPARATION TIME: *15 minutes*

YIELD: *1 – 2 servings*

2 tablespoons butter
⅛ cup finely chopped ham
2 tablespoons chopped onion
2 tablespoons chopped green pepper
⅛ cup sliced mushroom pieces
⅛ cup bleu cheese pieces
3 eggs, whipped
Dash water

1. Melt 1 tablespoon of the butter in a skillet or on a grill.

2. Combine ham, onion, pepper, mushrooms and bleu cheese. Place in skillet or grill and sauté until the cheese melts and combines with other ingredients.

3. Place to side of skillet or grill until ready to combine with eggs.

4. In separate dish, whip eggs and water.

5. Melt remaining tablespoon of butter in same skillet as vegetables. Pour eggs into skillet.

6. When eggs can be lifted to fold, add vegetables to center.

7. Fold egg sides into an omelet.

8. Serve immediately.

Janet Meyers Shockey '72 MEd EKEd

Learn to enjoy omelets with lots of steamed vegetables. Since eggs and cheese are high in cholesterol, "extend" the meal by "doubling up" on the veggies.

Cheese and Ham Souffles

PREPARATION TIME: *30 minutes plus overnight chilling and 45 minutes baking time*

YIELD: *6 sandwiches*

12 **slices bread, buttered on one side**	1. Cut crusts from bread.
6 **slices Old English cheese**	2. Place 6 slices of bread, buttered side down, in a greased 7 × 11-inch baking dish or pan.
6 **slices baked ham**	3. Place a slice of cheese and a slice of ham on each bread slice.
2 **cups milk**	4. Cover with remaining bread slices, buttered side up.
4 **eggs**	
1 **teaspoon salt**	5. Make a custard of milk, eggs, salt and paprika. Pour over bread.
1 **teaspoon paprika**	6. Refrigerate overnight or several hours.
½ **cup corn flakes, crushed**	7. When ready to bake, sprinkle with corn flakes and melted butter or margarine that have been mixed together.
2 **tablespoons butter or margarine, melted**	8. Bake at 350° for 45 minutes.
	9. Serve with mushroom sauce.

MUSHROOM SAUCE

2 **tablespoons butter or margarine**	1. Over medium heat melt butter or margarine, add flour to make a roux. Slowly add milk and cook until bubbly.
2 **tablespoons flour**	
1½ **cups milk**	
1 **teaspoon salt**	2. Add remaining ingredients and heat thoroughly.
¼ **teaspoon pepper**	
½ **pound sliced mushrooms, sautéed**	

This recipe can be doubled or halved easily.

Darlene Betar
Walter H. Betar '56 A&L

Spray pan with a non-stick coating and you won't need to butter the bread. Use skinned chicken or turkey instead of ham or blend the 2 meats. To lower cholesterol use skim milk and try 2 eggs plus 4 egg whites.

Baked Eggs

PREPARATION TIME: *1 hour 20 minutes*
YIELD: *8 – 12 servings*

2 cups grated sharp Cheddar cheese

¼ cup butter or margarine

1 cup light cream (or half and half)

1 teaspoon salt

½ teaspoon pepper

2 teaspoons mustard

12 eggs, slightly beaten

1. Spread cheese on bottom of 2 – 3 quart casserole. Cut butter and dot on top of cheese.

2. Combine cream, salt, pepper, and mustard. Pour half over cheese.

3. Pour in eggs. Pour rest of cream mixture over eggs.

4. Bake at 325° until knife inserted in center comes out clean, about 40 – 55 minutes.

5. For microwave, cook on low about 10 minutes, then turn and cook 5 – 10 minutes more or until knife inserted in center comes out clean.

"This is a favorite of mine when we have overnight guests for a game weekend. I prepare it Saturday night, bake it Sunday morning and serve with muffins and a fruit cup."

Judith Colbeck Roberts '61 AArt

A Curtiss-Wright engineering cadette of 1943 remembers: Each day a menu was posted for dinners in the Sandwich Shop in the basement of Old Main. The menu always offered "one egg any style" if you didn't like the evening's fare. This option was included even on the graduation banquet menu!

Cornmeal Eggs

PREPARATION TIME: *25 minutes*
YIELD: *6 servings*

1 cup cornmeal

1 cup boiling water

1 cup evaporated milk

¼ cup sifted flour

½ teaspoon salt

1 egg, well beaten

2 teaspoons baking powder

6 medium eggs

1. Place cornmeal in a mixing bowl, add hot water and let stand five minutes.

2. Add evaporated milk, flour, salt, beaten egg and baking powder to cornmeal mixture. Mix well.

3. Grease electric skillet or grill and heat to 400°.

4. Pour ½ cup batter in skillet then break one egg in the center of the batter.

5. Cover top with more batter. Brown bottom side, then turn over and brown other side, making sure egg is cooked. Serve with butter.

6. Repeat procedure for remaining batter and eggs.

Must serve immediately.

Frances L. Bechdel
Wayne R. Bechdel '43 HA

The Creamery employs thirteen full-time workers, four food science interns, and 25 students working part time.

Hungry Lion Breakfast Casserole

PREPARATION TIME: *1 hour plus overnight chilling time*
YIELD: *8 – 10 servings*

1 **pound bulk sausage, sweet or hot**	1. Crumble and brown sausage. Drain and allow to cool.
6 **eggs**	2. Butter a 9 × 13-inch glass baking dish and place sausage in bottom.
2 **cups milk**	
1 **teaspoon salt**	3. Beat eggs and milk together.
1 **teaspoon dry mustard**	4. Stir in remaining ingredients.
6 **slices bread, torn in small pieces**	5. Pour the milk and egg mixture over the sausage.
1½ **cups shredded sharp Cheddar cheese**	6. Cover tightly with foil or plastic wrap. Refrigerate overnight.
	7. Bake uncovered at 350° for 40 – 50 minutes.
	8. Allow to stand a few minutes before cutting.

Marlene M. Leslie '79 2LAS

Use your creativity to make this one different each time. Use meats, skim milk, whole grain bread and assorted cheeses. Steamed vegetables, like onions, green peppers, broccoli, may be layered.

Fiesta Bowl Enchilada Casserole

PREPARATION TIME: *1 hour 20 minutes*
YIELD: *8 – 10 servings*

2 – 3 (4 ounce) cans green chilies (not chopped or hot)

1 pound Cheddar cheese, grated

1 pound Monterey Jack cheese, grated

4 eggs, separated

1 (13 ounce) can evaporated milk

3 tablespoons flour

Salt and pepper, to taste

1. Remove seeds from chilies, wash, flatten and sliver.

2. Place half the chilies in bottom of 9 × 13-inch casserole.

3. Cover with Cheddar cheese.

4. Layer with the remaining chilies.

5. Cover with the Monterey Jack cheese.

6. Beat egg yolks with the evaporated milk, flour, salt and pepper. Set aside.

7. Beat egg whites until stiff.

8. Fold egg yolk mixture into egg whites.

9. Pour egg mixture over cheese and chilies.

10. Bake at 325° for 45 minutes to 1 hour.

Must serve immediately after baking. Can do ahead, up until the baking point.

Marion Lewis MacKinnon '48 Ed

The Creamery produces 25,000 pounds of Cheddar cheese a year.

Crusty Creamery Cheese Memories

PREPARATION TIME: *40 minutes*
YIELD: *4 servings*

Ingredients	Instructions
1 **refrigerator container of crusty French bread**	1. Lightly grease cookie sheet. Unroll bread into a rectangle on cookie sheet.
8 **ounces shredded mozzarella cheese**	2. Mix mozzarella cheese, ricotta cheese, pepper and parsley.
1 **pound ricotta cheese**	3. Place the cheese mixture on half the dough lengthwise.
1 **teaspoon black pepper**	
1 **tablespoon parsley**	4. Top cheese with sliced pepperoni or mushrooms or your favorite toppings. Fold over dough and seal edges.
2 **ounces sliced pepperoni (optional)**	5. Bake at 350° for 30 minutes.
8 **ounces sliced sautéed mushrooms (optional)**	
Black olives (optional)	
Fried peppers (optional)	

Serve plain or with your favorite spaghetti or pizza sauce.

Mardelle Sacco Kopnicky '64 HEc

For a "low-fat" version of this recipe use part-skim mozzarella cheese and low-fat ricotta.

Ice Cream Torte

PREPARATION TIME: *30 minutes plus 4 hours freezing time*
YIELD: *12 servings*

6 ounces semi-sweet chocolate chips	1. Melt chips in top of double boiler.
1 cup heavy cream	2. Stir in cream, coffee and liqueur. Set aside and let cool.
½ teaspoon instant coffee	3. Soften mocha ice cream.
1 tablespoon rum, cognac or brandy	4. Oil a 10 × 4-inch springform pan. Spread half of the cookie crumbs in pan. Cover with softened mocha ice cream.
1 quart mocha ice cream	
35 chocolate sandwich cookies, crushed	5. Spread remaining cookie crumbs on top of mocha ice cream.
1 quart dark chocolate ice cream	6. Drizzle half of the chocolate sauce on top and freeze until hardened.
½ pound English toffee, crushed	7. Soften dark chocolate ice cream and spread on top.
	8. Drizzle remaining sauce over top.
	9. Sprinkle toffee over sauce.
	10. Wrap in foil and freeze at least 4 hours.

Must do ahead.

Karen Bruno Ganter '71 CRS, '79 MEd CnEd

The Creamery serves approximately 300,000 ice cream cones and 125,000 dishes of ice cream per year.

Rum Raisin Ice Cream

PREPARATION TIME: *10 minutes plus overnight soaking of raisins and freezing time.*

YIELD: *½ gallon*

½ **cup raisins**	1. Soak raisins in rum overnight.
½ **cup dark rum**	2. Allow ice cream to soften and scoop into mixing bowl.
½ **gallon vanilla ice cream**	
¼ **teaspoon nutmeg**	3. Add rum, raisins and nutmeg, mix; rum will soften ice cream and make mixing easier.
	4. Place everything back into ice cream carton and refreeze.

Adjust ingredients for larger/smaller quantities or to taste.

This is an easy recipe that can be done ahead of time.

Larry Smarr

The Creamery makes 50-55 different flavors of ice cream.

Yogurt Yumsicles

PREPARATION TIME: *10 minutes plus freezing time*
YIELD: *7 – 8 popsicles*

2 cups vanilla yogurt

1 (6 ounce) can orange, pineapple or grape juice concentrate, thawed

1 (6 ounce) can water

1. Mix all ingredients together and pour into popsicle molds or small paper cups.

2. Place in freezer. Insert popsicle sticks or plastic spoons when mixture is partially frozen. Freeze until solid.

"These frozen confections are a big hit with my 2- and 5-year-old daughters and their friends. They also enjoy helping prepare them."

Alicia Peel Zilker '72 BiSc, '76 MS WLM

Use non-fat plain yogurt and add your own vanilla or other flavoring to make a low-calorie treat.

The Arts Festival weekend is the Creamery's busiest time of year. Football weekends run a close second.

A Little Breakfast
For a Few Friends

Mushroom Crust Quiche
or
Baked Eggs

Breakaway Coffee Cake
Whole Wheat Toast Strips
Canadian Bacon

Wedges of Fresh Melon
or
Touchdown Curried Fruit Bake

Coffee, Tea, Milk

Breads/Pasta

Most people are hooked on breads, biscuits, pastries and pasta!

Every meal is enhanced by the right bread . . . and often a lingering memory of the bread alone is the link to places visited and great times shared. Toasted, warmed, broiled, microwaved or cold, bread either sliced or whole, satisfies most of us.

When is the last time you brought some friends home to enjoy a counter full of your favorite homemade rolls, muffins, and breads with a pot of hot coffee? A cozy kitchen atmosphere featuring baked goods from your hearth almost insures your success as a host or hostess. Make the Breakaway Coffee Cake the focal point for a breakfast or brunch — build the rest of the meal around it!

Make a special occasion even more so by sending along a package of our Pecan Rolls or a loaf of Apple Butter Bread with your holiday dinner guests. Loaves of Irish Soda Bread or Crusty Old World Bread are a friendly way to say hello to a new neighbor.

Fruit butters dress up any bread. Simply whip together the butter with berries, peaches or any full-flavored fruits. Varieties of spreads for bread are equally delicious melted over hot pasta. Try butter flavored with parmesan cheese, garlic, onion, rosemary, dill, basil, parsley or crushed nuts.

Pasta is now served as frequently as potatoes once were. Hot or cold, it enjoys a coveted stature, as new recipes are developed continually to feature it in menus across the country. Why not feature pasta at your next party!

A Pasta Party Buffet

"Bring your favorite pasta to share with the group"

Our Chicken Lasagna or Spaghetti Pie could star at this event. Offer a crunchy garden salad, as most pasta main dishes are soft in texture and need something chewy or crunchy as a complement. A compote of fresh fruit with Mock Pralines or a chocolate dessert such as the Lion and the Mousse provide a lively finish. A glass of wine or iced tea works well with this prepare-ahead menu and for any pasta dishes your guests bring. Entertaining with a little help from your friends makes the party less work for you and is extra fun for everyone.

Crusty Old World Bread

PREPARATION TIME: *2 hours*
YIELD: *3 large loaves*

2 heaping tablespoons or 2 packages dry yeast

½ cup very hot tap water

1 teaspoon sugar

5 cups very hot tap water

2 tablespoons salt

⅓ cup salad oil

12½ – 13 cups flour (preferably high gluten flour or part whole wheat or rye or combination of all)

1. Soften yeast in ½ cup very hot tap water with sugar until it foams to top of cup.

2. Place 5 cups of very hot tap water, salt and oil into a large mixing bowl and gradually add 7 cups of flour, mix for about 3 minutes.

3. Add yeast to flour mixture and stir well.

4. Gradually add remaining flour until dough becomes quite stiff. Turn dough onto a floured board and knead until elastic and smooth (7 – 10 minutes).

5. Place dough in a large floured bowl and cover with a damp towel. Let rise until double in bulk, about 45 minutes to 1 hour in a warm place. Dough will rise at a cool temperature, but it will take longer.

6. Press out air bubbles and shape into three round or oblong loaves. Place on a well greased cookie sheet or a French bread pan.

7. Let loaves rise again about 30 minutes and if they lose their shape, press back into shape.

8. Bake at 400° for 15 minutes. Spray loaves with a water filled mister.

9. Reduce oven temperature to 350°. Repeat misting every 15 minutes until golden brown (about 50 – 60 minutes). Bread is done when it sounds hollow when tapped. Remove to wire racks. Cool thoroughly before storing.

"This bread freezes well for up to a month, but you should have a good, sharp, preferably serrated, knife for cutting."

Eleanor K. Wettstone
Eugene Wettstone '79 Honorary Alumnus

Quinn's Irish Soda Bread

PREPARATION TIME: *1 hour 30 minutes*
YIELD: *1 loaf*

½ cup butter, softened

½ cup sugar

2 eggs

½ cup sour cream

1 cup buttermilk

¼ teaspoon salt

1 teaspoon vanilla

2 teaspoons baking powder

1 teaspoon baking soda

1 cup raisins

4 cups flour

1. In large bowl mix butter and sugar with slotted spoon. Add eggs and mix well.

2. Add sour cream, buttermilk, salt and vanilla; mix well.

3. Add baking powder, baking soda and raisins; mix well after each addition.

4. Gradually add flour, mixing well after each addition. After last addition you might wish to mix with hands. Form into an oval shape and turn onto a greased and floured 9½ × 13-inch cookie sheet.

5. Bake at 375° for 1 hour. Remove to wire rack.

Linda Friedrichs Rowan '78 2LAS

In most recipes, you can substitute 2 egg whites for 1 egg and lower the cholesterol.

Old Forester's Black Bread

PREPARATION TIME: *1 hour 30 minutes*
YIELD: *1 loaf*

1½ **cups graham or rye flour**

2 **cups white flour**

2 **teaspoons baking soda**

½ **teaspoon salt**

½ **cup brown sugar**

½ **cup molasses**

2 **cups sour milk or buttermilk**

1. Mix all dry ingredients together.

2. Add molasses and milk, stir well.

3. Pour into a lightly greased 9 × 5 × 3-inch loaf pan.

4. Bake at 350° for 1 hour 10 minutes. Remove to wire rack.

You can also make 4 small loaves; bake for 30 minutes.

Joseph F. Gray '48 For

A College Bread-Baking Memory . . .

My sophomore year, I lived at University Terrace with four other women. Although the apartment was medium to large, the freezer space was small to non-existent. This recipe's main ingredient, bread dough, can be purchased in the freezer section of most grocery stores in State College. The package contains five or six frozen, uncooked loaves of white bread. To use a loaf, one can allow it to thaw overnight in the refrigerator or use a "quick method" by letting it thaw and rise in a warm oven (bread thaws in two to three hours).

I am a procrastinator by nature and after three or four of the loaves had sat in the freezer for almost two months, my roommates suggested I either bake them or throw them out. As luck would have it, this ultimatum came around finals and I was pressed for time. I decided to make all the loaves at once in a variety of different recipes and put them in the oven to rise at about 10 PM. (I had been planning an all-nighter, including cooking time on the agenda during study breaks.)

About the time my first study break rolled around (about 1 AM), I should have removed the bread from the oven and started cooking. I put down my notes and thought, "I'll just close my eyes for a minute before I get the dough."

I woke up at about 9:30 the next morning and on top of missing my first-and second-period classes, I discovered the oven was filled with goopy dough; it was even squeezing out the edges of the door and dripping onto the floor. So, I guess the moral of that story is, "don't try the 'quick' method unless you plan to stay awake to rescue the dough!"

Champion Dill Bread

PREPARATION TIME: *3 hours*
YIELD: *1 loaf*

1 **package active dry yeast**

¼ **cup warm water**

1 **cup sour cream**

1 **egg, beaten**

1 **tablespoon butter, softened**

1 **small onion, chopped**

2 **tablespoons sugar**

1 **tablespoon dill seed**

1 **tablespoon dill weed**

1 **teaspoon salt**

3 **cups flour**

1. In large mixing bowl sprinkle yeast over water.

2. Stir in sour cream, beaten egg, butter, onion, sugar, dill seed, dill weed, salt and one cup of flour. Blend well with spoon.

3. Add remaining flour, turn out on floured surface and knead until smooth.

4. Place in greased bowl, cover with cloth and let rise 90 minutes.

5. Punch down dough; divide into thirds.

6. Let rest 10 minutes.

7. Make each third into an 18-inch rope; braid the 3 pieces on a greased baking sheet.

8. Cover and let rise one hour.

9. Bake at 350° for 35 – 40 minutes.

Barbara Morrison Stahl '46 C&F
C. Drew Stahl '47, '49 MS, '54 PhD PNGE

Try substituting non-fat yogurt for sour cream. You save more than 200 calories.

Oatmeal Wheat Bread

PREPARATION TIME: *1 hour*
YIELD: *2 loaves*

2½ **cups whole wheat flour**

2½ **cups all-purpose flour**

1 **teaspoon salt**

1 **teaspoon sugar**

1 **package fast-acting dry yeast**

½ **cup molasses**

2¼ **cups milk**

¼ **cup margarine**

1 **cup oatmeal**

Oil

Margarine

1. Mix flours, salt, sugar and yeast in mixing bowl with dough hook.

2. Heat molasses, milk, margarine and oatmeal to 125°. Add to dry ingredients. Mix until dough pulls away from sides of bowl and forms a smooth ball. Add more all-purpose flour if necessary. Knead dough for 10 minutes or until a smooth elastic dough is formed.

3. Oil top of dough and let rise until doubled in bulk. Punch down and divide into 2 smooth balls, let rest, then shape into 2 loaves. Place in greased 9 × 5 × 3-inch loaf pans and let rise until doubled in bulk.

4. Rub top of loaves with margarine.

5. Bake at 375° for 40 minutes.

Kathryn E. Elkins '70 Nutr

The molasses provides extra iron for building healthy red blood cells. Use skim milk to reduce calories.

Boalsburg Banana Bread

PREPARATION TIME: *1 hour 10 minutes*
YIELD: *1 loaf*

3 large ripe bananas, mashed (1 cup)	1. Mash bananas and set aside.
1 cup sugar	2. Cream sugar and butter, then add eggs.
4 tablespoons butter	3. Mix together bananas and sugar-butter mixture.
2 eggs	
1½ cups flour	4. Combine flour, baking soda and salt.
1 teaspoon baking soda	5. Gradually stir flour mixture into the banana mixture.
¼ teaspoon salt	6. Pour into a 9 × 5 × 3-inch loaf pan.
	7. Bake at 375° for 50 minutes.
	8. Remove to wire rack.

Better if made a day ahead of serving.

"This recipe was adapted from my roommate's cookbook, when I was in summer school. It was a Sunday night, we were hungry, and the stores were closed. I checked the larder and found several ripe bananas, but no baking powder or milk. So I checked the cookbooks and found this banana bread recipe. That was 17 summers ago. It's now a family favorite and a great gift or party treat."

Marjory Brubaker Sente '73 Anthy

Try ½ cup sugar here with very ripe bananas. Speckled bananas have 88% sugar, while green or ripening ones range from 7 – 63% sugar.

Date and Nut Bread

PREPARATION TIME: *1 hour 45 minutes*
YIELD: *2 loaves*

1½ **cups dried raisins and chopped dates**

 2 **teaspoons baking soda**

1½ **cups sugar**

 ½ **cup butter or margarine**

1¾ **cups boiling water**

 2 **eggs, slightly beaten**

2½ **cups flour**

 1 **cup chopped nuts**

1. In medium bowl combine dried fruit, baking soda, sugar, and butter or margarine. Pour boiling water over and stir. Let cool.

2. When cool add slightly beaten eggs.

3. Add flour and blend well.

4. Stir in chopped nuts. Pour into 2 greased 9 × 5 × 3-inch pans.

5. Bake at 350° for 1 hour. Remove to wire rack.

"This is an old family recipe; I've been making it for 25 years and many Penn State friends have received the breads for the holidays or have found it on the menu at our Penn State football parties."

Roberta (Bobbi) Binder Aungst '66 MS SPA
Lester (Les) F. Aungst '61 MS CSpch, '65 PhD SPA

Try ¼ cup nuts. A cup of nuts has nearly 900 calories.

Lemon Apple Bread

PREPARATION TIME: *1 hour 10 minutes*

YIELD: *1 loaf*

2 cups flour	1. Mix flour, baking soda, baking powder, and salt in a small bowl.

2 cups flour

1 teaspoon baking soda

1 teaspoon baking powder

¾ teaspoon salt

¼ cup margarine

⅔ cup sugar

2 eggs, slightly beaten

2 cups coarsely shredded, peeled apples

4 teaspoons grated lemon peel

⅔ cup chopped nuts

1. Mix flour, baking soda, baking powder, and salt in a small bowl.

2. In a mixer bowl, cream margarine and sugar.

3. Beat eggs into margarine and sugar mixture.

4. Alternately add the flour mixture and the apples to the margarine, sugar and egg mixture, blending well after each addition.

5. By hand, stir in lemon peel and nuts.

6. Turn into a greased and floured 9 × 5 × 3-inch loaf pan.

7. Bake at 350° for 50 – 60 minutes. Remove to wire rack.

Bonnie Myers Tuten '69 LA

Save work and increase fiber by not peeling the apples.

Mocha Nut Bread

PREPARATION TIME: *30 minutes plus 55 minutes baking time*
YIELD: *1 loaf*

2 cups flour

1 cup sugar

½ cup cocoa

½ teaspoon baking soda

¼ teaspoon salt (optional)

3 heaping tablespoons instant coffee

1¼ cups sour cream

2 eggs, lightly beaten

⅓ cup melted butter

1 (6 ounce) package chocolate chips

½ cup chopped nuts (optional)

1. Sift together flour, sugar, cocoa, soda, salt and coffee.

2. Add dry ingredients to the sour cream, eggs and melted butter.

3. Add the chocolate chips and nuts. Mix well.

4. Pour batter into a greased and floured 9 × 5 × 3-inch loaf pan.

5. Bake at 350° for 50 – 55 minutes. Do not overbake.

Loaf is finished when top has glazed look and sides pull away from pan. Toothpick test may not work due to the chocolate chips.

Elizabeth A. Ennis '86 MBA

Substituting carob powder for cocoa and a grain cereal beverage like Postum for the coffee will lower the caffeine.

Pineapple Zucchini Bread

PREPARATION TIME: *30 minutes plus 1 hour baking time*
YIELD: *2 loaves*

3 **eggs**

2 **cups sugar**

2 **teaspoons vanilla**

1 **cup salad oil**

3 **cups flour**

1 **teaspoon baking powder**

1 **teaspoon baking soda**

1 **teaspoon salt**

2 **cups peeled and grated zucchini**

½ **cup raisins**

1 **cup crushed pineapple, drained**

1 **cup pecans, chopped**

1. Beat eggs, sugar, vanilla and oil until fluffy.

2. In separate bowl, sift together flour, baking powder, baking soda and salt. Set aside.

3. Add the zucchini to the egg mixture.

4. Next stir in the flour mixture. Mix well.

5. Add the raisins, pineapple and nuts.

6. Mix well by hand.

7. Pour into two greased and floured 9 × 5 × 3-inch loaf pans.

8. Bake at 350° for 1 hour. Remove to wire rack.

Judith Morgan

Buy unsweetened pineapple in its own juice and leave the skin on the zucchini.

Easy Raisin Bread

PREPARATION TIME: *1 hour 40 minutes*
YIELD: *1 loaf*

1 cup raisins	1. Combine raisins and baking soda in small bowl. Add boiling water. Cool 30 minutes.
1 teaspoon baking soda	
1 cup boiling water	
1½ cups all-purpose flour	2. Mix flour, sugar and salt in medium bowl.
½ cup sugar	3. Stir raisin mixture, egg and oil into flour mixture. Mix well.
½ teaspoon salt	
1 egg, beaten	4. Pour into a greased and floured 9 × 5 × 3-inch loaf pan.
1 tablespoon salad oil	5. Bake at 350° for 45 minutes, or until golden brown and when tester inserted in center comes out clean.
	6. Cool 10 minutes in pan. Remove to wire rack.

Serve warm with butter, margarine or cream cheese.

"This recipe is great to eat on the road to the football games."

LaRue (Dana) Herwick Forwood '68 HEEd

Serve with non-sugared apple butter or "all fruit" preserves.

Pepperoni Bread

PREPARATION TIME: *45 minutes plus 7 hours thawing time*
YIELD: *20 slices*

1 loaf frozen white bread dough

½ teaspoon vegetable shortening

¾ teaspoon fresh chopped parsley
  or parsley flakes

¾ teaspoon oregano

4 ounces thinly sliced pepperoni

2 cups shredded mozzarella
  cheese

1. Spread shortening over frozen dough. Place dough in a plastic bag and fasten. Let thaw and rise, usually 7 – 8 hours.

2. Remove bread from bag when ready and spread dough on a 10 × 15-inch no-stick cookie sheet. Sprinkle parsley and oregano over dough.

3. Cover dough entirely with sliced pepperoni leaving ¼-inch on each side uncovered. Top with mozzarella cheese.

4. Roll up lengthwise, jelly roll fashion. Pinch seams together. Place seam side down on cookie sheet and prick entire roll with knife for air holes.

5. Bake at 350° for 20 – 25 minutes until top and sides are golden brown.

6. Remove from oven and let set for 5 minutes. Cut into ¾-inch slices.

Also delicious reheated in microwave.

Gloria J. Sakal '81 CmpSc
Linda Sakal Deichert '78 Acctg

Penn State's bakery makes 246,000 loaves of bread a year.

Poppy Seed French Bread

PREPARATION TIME: *40 minutes*
YIELD: *1 loaf*

½ cup butter, melted

4 tablespoons chopped onion

1 tablespoon spicy mustard

2 teaspoons lemon juice

1 tablespoon poppy seed

½ teaspoon seasoned salt

1 (8 ounce) package Swiss cheese single slices

1 loaf French bread

1. Sauté all ingredients, except cheese and bread, until onion is tender.

2. Make thick cuts of bread, (not all the way through), in each cut insert cheese slices and spoon in sauce.

3. Wrap in foil.

4. Bake at 325° for 30 minutes.

Cut bread again (between slices of cheese) to make a sandwich effect and keep cheese on cut slices.

Elaine Christmas
William G. Christmas '48

The Penn State bakery uses approximately 585,000 pounds of flour and 52,000 dozen eggs a year.

Spicy Cheese-Olive Bread

PREPARATION TIME: *15 minutes*
YIELD: *1 loaf*

1 **(16 ounce) loaf unsliced French bread**

½ **cup butter or margarine, softened**

¼ **cup mayonnaise or Miracle Whip**

2 **cups (8 ounces) shredded mozzarella cheese**

½ **cup finely chopped green olives with pimentos**

1 **teaspoon garlic powder**

1 **teaspoon onion powder**

1. Cut French bread in half lengthwise.

2. Combine butter and mayonnaise; stir in remaining ingredients.

3. Spread mixture on cut side of bread.

4. Bake uncovered at 350° for 10 – 15 minutes.

"This recipe is one of my most popular. No matter how much I make for a party or barbecue I always run out."

Can combine all ingredients in bowl the day before. Slice and spread on bread shortly before baking.

Susan Loadman Ingram '75 MERC

Use part-skim mozzarella cheese to keep fat intake low.

Best-Ever Bran Muffins

PREPARATION TIME: *25 minutes plus 12 hours chilling time*
YIELD: *5 dozen muffins*

1 cup vegetable shortening	1. In large bowl cream together shortening and honey.
2 cups honey	
4 eggs	2. Beat in eggs.
2 cups Kellogg's All-Bran cereal	3. Stir in cereals and add boiling water.
4 cups Nabisco 100% Bran cereal	4. In separate bowl sift together flour, baking soda and salt. Add to batter and mix well.
1½ cups boiling water	
5 cups flour	5. Mix in buttermilk.
5 teaspoons baking soda	6. Refrigerate at least 12 hours or overnight.
2 teaspoons salt	
1 quart buttermilk	7. Pour into greased muffin tins or paper liners.
	8. Bake at 400° for 20 minutes or until done. Remove to wire rack.

Microwave directions: Use a 6-cup muffin pan with 2 paper cups in each. Fill half full. Microwave on high, 2 ½ – 3 minutes.

This batter may be kept in a covered container in the refrigerator for as long as 6 weeks. (Bake half a dozen fresh for breakfast.)

Bess Treager Clarke '40 HEc

Penn State's bakery makes 135,000 dozen donuts a year.

214

Snacking Muffins

PREPARATION TIME: *1 hour*
YIELD: *12 muffins*

1 cup sifted white flour

¾ cup whole wheat flour

2½ teaspoons baking powder

½ teaspoon cinnamon

¼ teaspoon nutmeg

⅓ cup margarine

⅓ cup brown sugar

2 eggs

⅔ cup milk

⅔ cup chopped apples

⅔ cup chopped walnuts

¼ cup raisins

Wheat germ

1. In mixing bowl, combine flours, baking powder and spices.

2. In second bowl, cream margarine, brown sugar and eggs until smooth.

3. Add milk and flour mixture alternately to creamed mixture, stirring after each addition.

4. Blend in apples, walnuts and raisins.

5. Spoon batter into buttered or paper-lined muffin tins, about ⅔ full. Sprinkle lightly with wheat germ.

6. Bake at 375° for 25 minutes or until tops are golden brown.

James D. Pyles '87 Mktg

Use skim milk and vary with other fruits and nuts for a change.

Blue and White Muffins From Colvmns By the Sea

PREPARATION TIME: *35 minutes*
YIELD: *20 muffins*

½ cup butter, softened

1 cup sugar

2 eggs

1 cup lemon yogurt

1 teaspoon vanilla

2 cups flour

1 teaspoon baking soda

1 teaspoon baking powder

2 teaspoons cinnamon (optional)

2 cups fresh or frozen blueberries

1. Cream butter and sugar.

2. Add eggs, yogurt and vanilla; mix with electric mixer.

3. In a separate bowl mix flour, baking soda, baking powder and cinnamon with a fork.

4. Stir flour mixture into yogurt mixture and fold in blueberries.

5. Fill greased or paper-lined muffin tins ⅔ full.

6. Bake at 375° for 20 minutes or until golden.

7. Cool in tins for 10 minutes, then remove to wire rack.

"The guests at our Inn love these best warm, especially the Penn Staters."

Catherine Shultz Rein '64 LMR
Barry Rein '62 Chem

Non-fat yogurt helps keep calories down. Add 1 teaspoon lemon juice or a few drops lemon extract to plain non-fat yogurt.

Banana Paws

PREPARATION TIME: *30 minutes*
YIELD: *12 muffins*

2 cups flour

½ cup sugar

2 teaspoons baking powder

½ teaspoon baking soda

½ teaspoon salt

¼ teaspoon cinnamon

½ cup (1 large) banana, mashed

½ cup milk

⅓ cup salad oil

1 egg, slightly beaten

1. Line muffin pans with paper baking cups or grease (not oil) the pans.

2. In medium bowl, combine flour, sugar, baking powder, baking soda, salt and cinnamon.

3. Stir in banana, milk, oil and egg until dry ingredients are moistened.

4. Spoon batter into prepared muffin cups, filling ⅔ full.

5. Bake at 375° for 15 – 20 minutes or until golden brown.

6. Remove from pan immediately. Serve warm.

Mark L. Eakman '80 PM

Try substituting 1 cup whole wheat flour and 1 cup white, skim milk and 2 egg whites for 1 egg.

French Breakfast Muffins

PREPARATION TIME: *25 minutes*
YIELD: *36 mini muffins*

1½ **cups plus 2 tablespoons flour**

¾ **cup sugar**

2 **teaspoons baking powder**

¼ **teaspoon salt**

¼ **teaspoon ground nutmeg**

½ **cup milk**

1 **egg, beaten**

⅓ **cup butter, melted**

½ **teaspoon vanilla**

½ **cup butter, melted**

1 **teaspoon cinnamon**

½ **cup sugar**

1. Combine flour, sugar, baking powder, salt and ground nutmeg.

2. Add milk, egg and ⅓ cup melted butter. Mix thoroughly.

3. Grease and flour 3 small muffin pans (tassie pans) or line with paper baking cups.

4. Fill ½ full.

5. Bake at 400° for 10 minutes or until lightly browned.

6. While muffins are baking, combine vanilla and ½ cup melted butter.

7. In a separate bowl combine cinnamon and ½ cup sugar.

8. When muffins are baked, remove from pan immediately and roll first in butter-vanilla mixture then roll in cinnamon-sugar mixture.

Susan Young Henning '63 HEc
George T. Henning Jr. '63 A&L

Use part whole wheat flour, skim milk and less sugar on top for extra-healthy muffins.

Pecan Rolls

PREPARATION TIME: *4 – 5 hours (including rising time)*
YIELD: *2 dozen rolls*

1 **package active dry yeast**

½ **cup lukewarm water**

1 **cup mashed potatoes**

½ **cup sugar**

2 **teaspoons salt**

⅔ **cup margarine**

1 **cup milk, scalded**

2 **eggs, beaten**

6 **or more cups flour**

Margarine

Brown sugar

Cinnamon

GLAZE MIXTURE

1 **cup brown sugar**

½ **cup margarine**

¼ **cup light corn syrup**

Pecans as desired

1. Dissolve yeast in warm water.

2. Add potatoes, sugar, salt and margarine to hot milk and allow to cool. Add dissolved yeast and beaten eggs to cooled milk mixture and mix well.

3. Add enough flour to make a soft dough. Knead well for 8 – 10 minutes, adding flour until dough is smooth.

4. Place dough in greased bowl. Cover and let rise until double in bulk. Divide dough into 2 parts. Roll each part into a rectangle.

5. Spread with margarine, brown sugar, and sprinkle with cinnamon. Roll up jelly-roll style and slice about 1″ thick. (Use a piece of thread, wrap it around and pull.)

6. Prepare glaze mixture.

1. Place all ingredients in a pan, mix and heat. Put half of the glaze in a 9 × 13-inch pan, put the other half in a second 9 × 13-inch pan.

2. Place rolls on top of glaze about ½ inch apart. Let rise until double.

3. Bake at 375° for 30 minutes.

4. Remove from oven and invert pan to remove rolls and cool.

Kay Greb Gasowski '72 SecEd

Use part whole wheat flour to increase the fiber.

"Stickies"

PREPARATION TIME: *20 minutes plus 30 minutes cooking time plus thawing time for dough*

YIELD: *9 rolls*

1 loaf frozen dough	1. Grease dough with shortening and thaw by placing it in plastic bag or plastic wrap. (The purpose is only to thaw dough, not to let it rise.)
Solid shortening	
2 tablespoons butter	2. Melt 2 tablespoons butter in 9 × 9 × 2-inch aluminum pan on top of stove. Remove from heat.
¼ cup packed light brown sugar	3. Mix in ¼ cup packed light brown sugar and molasses with a fork until moist and smooth. (Mixture should be thick and wet. If too thin, add more brown sugar until desired consistency is obtained.)
2 tablespoons dark molasses	
4 tablespoons butter, softened	4. Press mixture with a fork to cover bottom of pan. Set aside.
½ cup light brown sugar	5. Roll thawed dough into a 9 × 9-inch square.
Cinnamon to taste	6. Spread dough with softened butter, covering entire surface.
	7. Sprinkle ½ cup light brown sugar over buttered area.
	8. Top with cinnamon to desired taste.
	9. Roll up jelly-roll style. Cut into 9 pieces. Place pieces in prepared pan.
	10. Cover and allow to rise in warm place for about 1 hour, or until buns reach top of pan.
	11. Bake at 375° for 25 – 30 minutes or until golden brown.
	12. Remove from oven and let cool for 5 minutes.
	13. Place serving plate, upside down, on top of pan and flip stickies onto plate.

Laura A. Blackburn '85 CmDis

Old World Coffee Cake

PREPARATION TIME: *1 hour 30 minutes*
YIELD: *1 coffee cake*

¾ **cup shortening**

1 **cup plus 2 tablespoons sugar**

1½ **teaspoons vanilla**

4 **eggs**

3 **cups sifted flour**

1½ **teaspoons baking soda**

1½ **teaspoons baking powder**

¾ **teaspoon salt (optional)**

1½ **cups sour cream**

1. Grease and flour an angel food cake pan. Line bottom with waxed paper.

2. Cream shortening and sugar together; add vanilla and mix until well blended.

3. Add eggs one at a time, beating well after each addition.

4. Sift together flour, baking soda, baking powder and salt. Add to creamed mixture alternately with the sour cream.

5. Spread half of the batter in the prepared pan.

6. Prepare the filling.

FILLING

6 **tablespoons margarine**

1 **cup firmly packed brown sugar**

2 **teaspoons cinnamon**

1 **cup coarsely chopped walnuts**

1. Cream margarine and brown sugar; add cinnamon and chopped nuts. Mix with fork until crumbly.

2. Spread half of the filling over the batter.

3. Cover with remaining batter.

4. Sprinkle remaining filling over top of batter.

5. Bake at 350° for 50 – 60 minutes or until toothpick inserted in cake comes out clean.

Joan E. Sexton '81 Admin, '86 MS PhEd

Penn State's food service operation serves 30,000 pounds of granola a year.

Tailgaters' Coffee Cake

PREPARATION TIME: *1 hour 30 minutes*
YIELD: *1 coffee cake*

½ cup shortening

¾ cup sugar

1 teaspoon vanilla

3 eggs

2 cups flour

1 teaspoon baking powder

1 teaspoon baking soda

1 cup sour cream

6 tablespoons butter, softened

1 cup brown sugar, packed

2 teaspoons cinnamon

1 cup chopped nuts

1. Cream shortening, sugar and vanilla. Add eggs and beat well.

2. Sift flour with baking powder and soda. Add to creamed mixture, alternating with sour cream. Spread half of the batter in a greased and floured 10-inch tube pan.

3. Cream butter, brown sugar and cinnamon. Add nuts and mix well to make topping mixture. Dot batter in pan with half of topping mixture, cover with remaining batter and sprinkle top with remaining topping mixture.

4. Bake at 350° for 50 minutes.

Karen D. Watson '87 Fin

Save calories by cutting sugar and nuts each to ½ cup in the topping mixture.

During the breakfast rush or after the downtown bars close, 25-30 stickies come out of the Diner's kitchen every minute.

Tailgate Sour Cream Coffee Cake

PREPARATION TIME: *1 hour 15 minutes*
YIELD: *1 coffee cake*

1 cup shortening (½ margarine and ½ butter)

1¼ cups sugar

2 eggs

1 cup sour cream

2 cups flour

½ teaspoon baking soda

1½ teaspoons baking powder

1 teaspoon vanilla

TOPPING

¾ cup chopped nuts (pecans or walnuts)

1 teaspoon cinnamon

2 tablespoons sugar

1. In a large bowl, cream shortening, sugar and eggs.

2. Add sour cream and mix well.

3. Gradually add remaining ingredients until well blended.

4. Pour half of the batter into a greased and floured bundt or angel food pan.

5. Layer half of the topping on batter in pan, add remaining batter and topping.

6. Bake at 350° for 55 minutes.

1. In a small bowl mix all ingredients together. Sprinkle between layers and on top of coffee cake.

Joan Burlein Michelotti '51 MedT

Penn State's bakery makes 275,000 dozen rolls a year.

Crumb Coffee Cake

PREPARATION TIME: *1 hour*
YIELD: *1 coffee cake*

1½ cups flour

1½ teaspoons baking powder

Pinch of salt

1 cup brown sugar

¼ cup margarine

¼ cup vegetable shortening

1 egg

½ cup milk

½ teaspoon vanilla

1. Sift flour, baking powder, and salt together. Add brown sugar.

2. Using a pastry blender, cut shortening and margarine into dry ingredients. Reserve ½ cup of this crumb mixture for topping.

3. In a separate bowl beat egg well. Blend in vanilla and milk.

4. Make a "well" in dry ingredients. Pour liquid mixture into "well".

5. Stir only until flour mixture is moistened. Do not over-beat; batter will look lumpy.

6. Pour into a greased 8 × 8-inch square cake pan and top with reserved ½ cup crumb mixture.

7. Bake at 375° for 25 minutes.

Jean Craumer Persson '47 HEEd

Decrease the sugar to ½ cup and use skim milk to lower the calories.

Breakaway Coffee Cake

PREPARATION TIME: *2½ hours*
YIELD: *24 servings*

½ **cup warm water**	1. Dissolve yeast in warm water.
2 **packages dry yeast**	2. Stir in milk, sugar, salt, eggs, shortening, and half of flour. Mix well.
1½ **cups lukewarm milk**	3. Add remaining flour one cup at a time until dough is no longer sticky.
½ **cup sugar**	
2 **teaspoons salt**	4. Turn onto a lightly floured board and knead until smooth.
2 **eggs**	
½ **cup shortening**	5. Place dough in a greased bowl and cover with a damp cloth. Let rise in a warm place for 1½ hours.
6 – 7 **cups pastry flour**	
½ **cup butter**	6. Punch dough down and let rise again for 30 minutes.
1½ **cups brown sugar**	7. Melt ½ cup butter; set aside.
3 **teaspoons cinnamon**	8. Combine brown sugar and cinnamon; set aside.

1. Dissolve yeast in warm water.

2. Stir in milk, sugar, salt, eggs, shortening, and half of flour. Mix well.

3. Add remaining flour one cup at a time until dough is no longer sticky.

4. Turn onto a lightly floured board and knead until smooth.

5. Place dough in a greased bowl and cover with a damp cloth. Let rise in a warm place for 1½ hours.

6. Punch dough down and let rise again for 30 minutes.

7. Melt ½ cup butter; set aside.

8. Combine brown sugar and cinnamon; set aside.

9. Break off bite-size pieces of raised dough.

10. Barely coat dough pieces with butter and roll in cinnamon sugar mixture.

11. Spray 2 bundt pans with vegetable spray and layer coated balls in pan until about ½ to ¾ full.

12. Cover with cloth and let rise until dough balls reach the top of pan.

13. Bake at 400° for 20 minutes.

14. Remove from oven and turn over immediately onto a plate.

Can double or halve easily.

Eloise J. O'Brien '82 SoSc

Use less salt, some whole wheat pastry flour and less brown sugar.

225

Spaghetti Pie

PREPARATION TIME: *1 hour*
YIELD: *4 – 6 servings*

6 ounces spaghetti

2 tablespoons butter

⅓ cup Parmesan cheese

2 eggs, beaten

1 pound ground beef

½ cup chopped onions

¼ cup chopped green peppers

8 ounces tomato sauce

6 ounces tomato paste

1 teaspoon sugar

1 teaspoon oregano

½ teaspoon garlic salt

1 cup cottage cheese

½ cup shredded mozzarella cheese

1. Cook spaghetti. Drain. Stir in butter, Parmesan cheese, and eggs. Form mixture into crust in a greased 10-inch pie pan.

2. In skillet, cook beef, onions, and peppers until tender and brown. Drain fat.

3. Stir in tomato sauce and paste, sugar, oregano, and garlic salt. Simmer 15 minutes.

4. Spread crust with cottage cheese and cover with sauce mixture. Bake uncovered at 350° for 20 minutes.

5. Sprinkle with mozzarella cheese and bake 5 – 10 minutes more.

Marta-Jo Prinkey Nicol '74 RehEd

When making recipes ahead, refrigerate cooked ground beef with some water so that all extra fat will "surface" and can be skimmed.

Chicken Lasagna

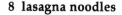

PREPARATION TIME: *50 minutes plus 40 minutes cooking time*
YIELD: *12 – 14 servings*

8	**lasagna noodles**
½	**cup chopped onion**
3	**tablespoons margarine**
1	**(10½ ounce) can cream of chicken soup**
1	**(6 ounce) can sliced mushrooms**
⅓	**cup milk**
1	**teaspoon parsley**
1½	**cups regular cottage cheese**
2½	**cups cooked chicken, torn into small pieces**
1	**cup shredded Cheddar cheese**
1	**cup shredded mozzarella cheese**
	Parmesan cheese

1. Cook noodles until almost done; drain and set aside.

2. In medium saucepan sauté onions in margarine until tender.

3. Add soup, mushrooms, milk, and parsley.

4. In a 9 × 13-inch baking pan layer half of the noodles and top with half of the sauce, cottage cheese, chicken, and all the Cheddar cheese.

5. Repeat layers this time ending with all the mozzarella cheese.

6. Sprinkle top lightly with Parmesan cheese.

7. Bake at 350° for 40 minutes.

8. Let cool 10 minutes before serving.

May be microwaved for 12 minutes at 80% power.

Barbara E. Gillis
George Gillis '68 2DDT

Use whole-grain lasagna for more fiber. Try substituting low-fat dairy products like skim milk, low-fat cottage cheese and part-skim mozzarella for fewer calories.

Lion's Share Lasagna

PREPARATION TIME: *3 – 4 hours cooking time for the sauce*
YIELD: *6 – 8 servings*

SAUCE

1	**tablespoon shortening**
¾	**pound beef roast, cut in chunks**
½	**pound sweet sausage**
1	**small onion, chopped**
2	**cloves garlic, minced**
2	**tablespoons basil**
2	**tablespoons oregano**
2	**cups water**
2	**(12 ounce) cans tomato paste**

1. Melt shortening in large pot.
2. Add beef and sausage and cook slowly until browned.
3. Add onion and garlic and cook until golden.
4. Add basil, oregano and water (more water if necessary to cover the meat). Bring to a boil.
5. Add tomato paste and stir.
6. Lower heat and simmer at least 3 hours.
7. When sauce is done, remove any large chunks of meat.

LASAGNA

12	**cooked lasagna noodles**
16	**ounces ricotta cheese**
8	**ounces mozzarella cheese**
	Freshly grated Parmesan cheese (at least 5 ounces)

1. In deep rectangular baking pan place a few spoonfuls of sauce.
2. Cover this with a layer of lasagna noodles, followed by dabs of ricotta cheese, slices of mozzarella, and Parmesan cheese. Top with ⅓ of the sauce.
3. Repeat layers.
4. The last layer should be only lasagna, Parmesan cheese and sauce.
5. Bake uncovered at 350° for 15 – 20 minutes.
6. Remove from oven and let stand 5 – 10 minutes before cutting and serving.

Meat removed from sauce earlier can be served as a side dish.

Charlotte Brown Zarfoss '64 EKEd
Thomas F. Zarfoss '65 A&A

Ricotta cheese is sold in a low-fat version.

228

Lion Lovers' Lasagna (Meatless)

PREPARATION TIME: *1 hour 30 minutes*
YIELD: *8 – 12 servings*

¼ cup chopped onions

¼ cup butter or margarine

¼ cup flour

2 teaspoons instant chicken or vegetable bouillon

1 teaspoon garlic powder

¼ teaspoon thyme

¼ teaspoon pepper

2½ cups skim milk

1½ cups low-fat cottage cheese, drained

2 (10 ounce) packages frozen chopped broccoli, thawed and drained

2 (8 ounce) cans mushroom pieces, drained

9 lasagna noodles, cooked

3 cups shredded Swiss cheese

1. Sauté onion in butter or margarine in a large skillet. Stir in flour, bouillon, garlic powder, thyme and pepper. Cook until smooth and bubbly. Gradually add milk. Cook until sauce boils and thickens, stirring constantly.

2. Stir in cottage cheese, broccoli and mushrooms.

3. In an ungreased 9 × 13-inch pan spread 1 cup of the sauce mixture. Layer ⅓ of the noodles, 2 cups sauce and 1 cup cheese. Repeat layering twice.

4. Bake at 350° for 25 – 35 minutes.

5. Let stand 15 minutes before serving.

Natalie A. Updegrove '84 Nutr

This is lower in fat than most lasagna recipes. Mixing part-skim mozzarella with the Swiss cheese will decrease fat further.

Parmesan Chicken With Pasta

PREPARATION TIME: *1 hour*
YIELD: *4 – 6 servings*

3 whole chicken breasts	1. Bone, skin, and flatten chicken breasts with mallet. Season with salt and pepper and coat in flour.
Salt and pepper	
Flour	
6 tablespoons butter	2. Melt butter over medium heat and sauté chicken on both sides. Remove chicken from skillet and place in a 9 × 13-inch casserole dish.
1 cup mushrooms, sliced	
½ cup light cream	3. Sauté mushrooms in remaining butter and place over chicken. Pour cream around chicken and sprinkle with Parmesan cheese.
½ cup freshly grated Parmesan cheese	
	4. Bake at 350° for 12 minutes. Serve with pasta.

PASTA

½ cup chopped onion	1. Sauté onion in butter. Add pasta and stir for 2 minutes. Add vermouth and stir until liquid is absorbed. Add chicken broth and simmer for about 15 minutes.
3 tablespoons butter	
1½ cups orzo (small rice-shaped pasta)	
¼ cup vermouth	
2 cups chicken broth	

The secret to success is the slow cooking. A great recipe for entertaining.

Orzo is not a brand name but a type of pasta. For this recipe to work, you must use orzo. It is widely available in most supermarkets.

Susan Rode McLaughlin '72 IFS

Skinned chicken breasts are much lower in fat than non-skinned chicken breasts. When making your own chicken broth or using canned, refrigerate several hours or overnight and then skim off to decrease unwanted fat.

Lanza Vegetarian Casserole

PREPARATION TIME: *1 hour 30 minutes plus 1 hour cooking*
YIELD: *6 servings*

SAUCE

1 tablespoon olive oil

1 clove garlic

1 (12 ounce) can tomato paste

1 (28 ounce) can diced tomatoes with puree

2 cups water (use more if you like a thinner sauce)

½ cup chopped fresh parsley

Salt and pepper to taste

½ teaspoon chopped basil

1 teaspoon sugar

1. Warm olive oil in Dutch oven.

2. Add whole clove of garlic. Sauté until golden (not brown).

3. Discard garlic.

4. Add remaining ingredients. Bring to a boil and simmer for one hour.

VEGETABLES

1 tablespoon olive oil

6 – 8 mushrooms, diced

1 green pepper, diced

1 red pepper, diced

1 medium zucchini, diced

1 small onion, diced

1 clove garlic, pressed

1 (4 ounce) jar diced pimentos

15 chopped spinach leaves

⅔ (16 ounce) package spinach noodles or fettucine

8 ounces mozzarella cheese, grated

½ cup Parmesan cheese, grated

1. Sauté mushrooms, green pepper, red pepper, zucchini, and onion in olive oil.

2. Add garlic, pimentos, and spinach leaves. Cook, uncovered for about 3 minutes. Drain well.

3. Cook noodles and drain.

4. Spray 7 × 12-inch pan with spray shortening.

5. Spread pasta in pan. Top with cooked vegetables and about 1½ cups tomato sauce.

6. Add 6 ounces grated mozzarella cheese. Top with remaining sauce.

7. Bake, covered at 325° for 40 minutes.

8. Uncover and add remaining mozzarella and Parmesan cheese.

9. Bake uncovered at 375° for 15 minutes.

Can use bottled sauce. Cuts preparation time by one hour.

Nancy Brebner Mastroianni '57 A&L
George A. Mastroianni '57 A&L

Desserts

There is no question about the popularity of desserts!

Happy Valley memories for many include celebrating a roommate's birthday with chocolate cake at the Corner Room; collapsing after finals with a piece of Tavern Cheese Cake; or making sure you didn't miss dinner at the dining hall when PSU-Style Fudge Pudding or Midnight Cake was on the menu.

"Care packages" from home often included your mother's best, like Peanut Butter Fudge Brownies or a pan of wonderful bar cookies that disappeared the day they arrived! The next time you visit your collegiates, treat them to a tray of Zucchini Bars with Caramel Frosting.

Few Penn State experiences are as nostalgic as relishing ice cream cones from the Creamery. Today, new flavors like Keeney Beaney chocolate and Peachy Paterno are wonderful to take home packed in dry ice. You might have fun experimenting with Ice Cream Torte by substituting your favorite Penn State Creamery flavors.

Whether your meal is formal or casual, **Cookin' With The Lion** offers desserts by the dozens to suit your needs and please your palate. Health-and weight-conscious cooks, who are reluctant to give up their sweet finale, will be able to adapt our desserts to meet their requirements by following our nutrition tips.

As you try to choose your dessert from all included here, remember that *contrast* within the menu is a good guideline. If your supper is cold chicken and a fruit salad, an appealing contrast for dessert is our warm Nittany Bread Pudding Souffle. When heavy courses precede dessert, select sorbets or sherbets, or any fresh fruit in its beautiful natural state or lightly poached in wine.

If you or your guests have an unrelenting sweet tooth regardless of what went before dessert, then go ahead and have your rich indulgence, such as Toll House Pie, but serve small portions! A thoughtful host or hostess offers both fruit and a sweet dessert.

Finally, for those of you who love to give gifts made in your kitchen or who like to offer chocolates to your guests after a meal, try the ultimate in confections, Raspberry Truffles or Lion Butter fudge.

Marianne Neiderberg's Tailgate Cake

PREPARATION TIME: *1 hour 30 minutes*

YIELD: *1 bundt cake*

1 2-layer yellow cake mix

2 (4 ounce) packages of instant vanilla pudding

½ cup milk

½ cup salad oil

1 cup whiskey, amaretto, or rum

4 large eggs

1. Blend cake mix and pudding mix together.

2. In separate bowl, blend milk, oil and liquor; add dry cake and pudding mix. Beat in eggs, one at a time. Mix for two minutes; scrape sides of bowl often and beat until smooth.

3. Pour into non-stick, lightly greased bundt or tube pan. Bake as directed on box or at 325° for 60 – 70 minutes until lightly browned. Cake is done when an inserted toothpick comes out clean.

GLAZE

½ cup butter

1 cup sugar

1 tablespoon water

1 cup amaretto

1. Melt butter in sauce pan. Add sugar, water and 1 tablespoon amaretto. Bring to a light boil and simmer for 10 – 15 minutes.

2. Remove from heat, let cool three minutes and stir in remaining amaretto.

3. When cake is done, remove from oven and pour glaze over cake in pan. Let cool on rack for one hour. Remove cake from pan and place on plate. *Cake is best if left to mellow at least two days before cutting.*

VARIATION: Mix equal amounts of roasted almonds and brown sugar together. Sprinkle on bottom of greased cake pan. Be careful not to sprinkle on side of cake pan. Once cake mix is prepared, pour gently into pan. Make sure almond and brown sugar mix does not splash up into batter when pouring cake into pan.

Frances Neidigh Sowko '50
Raymond C. Sowko '50 Ed

234

Applesauce Cake

PREPARATION TIME: *1 hour 30 minutes*
YIELD: *1 cake*

2 cups sugar

½ cup shortening

2 eggs

2½ cups flour

¼ teaspoon baking powder

1½ teaspoons baking soda

1½ teaspoons salt

¾ teaspoon cinnamon

½ teaspoon cloves

½ cup water

1½ cups applesauce

½ cup chopped walnuts

1 cup raisins or dates

FROSTING

1 cup brown sugar

½ cup butter

¼ cup milk

2 cups sifted powdered sugar

½ teaspoon vanilla

1. Cream sugar, shortening and eggs.

2. Add flour, baking powder, soda, salt, cinnamon, cloves and water. Mix well.

3. Add applesauce and beat for two minutes.

4. Fold in walnuts and raisins or dates. Pour into a greased and floured 9 × 13-inch cake pan or two 8-inch round cake pans.

5. Bake at 350° for 60 – 65 minutes for a rectangular pan; or 50 – 55 minutes for round pans. It's done when a toothpick inserted in center comes out clean..

6. Remove from pans and cool; frost with a brown sugar frosting.

1. In medium saucepan melt brown sugar and butter. Heat for 2 minutes.

2. Add milk and cook until boiling. Cool.

3. Add powdered sugar and vanilla. Beat by hand until smooth.

Sheryl J. May '80 MuEd

Unsweetened applesauce is available as a lower-sugar alternative to regular.

Easy Apple Cake

PREPARATION TIME: *50 minutes*

YIELD: *9 servings*

1 **cup sugar**

1 **cup flour**

1 **teaspoon baking soda**

1 **teaspoon cinnamon**

½ **teaspoon nutmeg**

¼ **cup butter, melted**

1 **egg**

2 **tablespoons hot water**

2½ **cups unpeeled cubed apples**

½ **cup nuts**

1. In large bowl combine sugar, flour, baking soda, cinnamon, nutmeg, butter, egg and water. Mix until blended.

2. Stir in apples and nuts.

3. Spread into a greased 8- or 9-inch square pan.

4. Bake at 350° for 35 – 40 minutes.

Sharon M. Mlodoch '77 Math

Try a sweet variety of apples and you can cut the sugar in half.

Blue Band Special Chocolate Cake

PREPARATION TIME: *1 hour*
YIELD: *1 three-layer cake*

1 cup margarine

2 cups sugar

3 eggs

2½ cups flour

½ cup cocoa

2 teaspoons baking soda

2 teaspoons baking powder

1 teaspoon salt

1 cup milk

1 cup boiling water

1 teaspoon vanilla

1. Grease and flour three 9-inch round cake pans.

2. Cream margarine and sugar. Add eggs, one at a time, beat well after each addition.

3. Sift dry ingredients together. Alternate adding milk and creamed mixture to dry ingredients.

4. After batter is well blended, add boiling water and vanilla.

5. Bake at 350° for 30 – 35 minutes.

6. Cool and frost with chocolate butter cream frosting.

FROSTING

⅓ cup soft margarine

⅛ teaspoon salt

3 cups powdered sugar (sift if lumpy)

3 squares (1 ounce each) unsweetened chocolate, melted

¼ cup milk

1½ teaspoons vanilla

1. Beat margarine, salt and 1 cup powdered sugar until light and fluffy.

2. Blend in melted chocolate.

3. Add remaining sugar alternating with milk and vanilla. Mix until smooth and creamy. (For good spreading consistency you may need to add more sugar to thicken or milk to thin frosting.)

"This cake is a long-time family favorite. It was renamed for our daughter, Karen, a marching Blue Band member from 1979 to 1982."

Rosanne Gonzales Grapsy '58 BA

Corner Room Chocolate Cake

PREPARATION TIME: *1 hour 10 minutes*
YIELD: *1 cake*

2½ cups sifted cake flour

½ teaspoon salt

1 teaspoon baking soda

3 squares unsweetened chocolate

1 cup butter

2 cups sugar

5 eggs

1 teaspoon vanilla

1 cup buttermilk

1 tablespoon hot water

1. Have all ingredients at room temperature. Sift together flour, salt and baking soda. Set aside.

2. Melt chocolate over boiling water; cool.

3. Cream butter with an electric mixer until light; gradually add sugar and beat until light and fluffy.

4. Blend in eggs, one at a time, beat well after each addition. Add vanilla. Blend in cooled chocolate and beat until well blended.

5. Add sifted dry ingredients alternating with buttermilk to creamed mixture. Blend thoroughly after each addition.

6. Add water and mix just enough to combine. Pour batter into 2 greased and floured 9-inch round cake pans.

7. Bake at 375° for 30 – 40 minutes or until cake tester comes out clean.

When cool, frost with a rich fudge frosting.

"The Corner Room was a popular place to visit during class breaks or after the movies, etc. This cake was a special favorite. In 1954 or 1955 the recipe was published in News and Views, *the newsletter of the College of Home Economics."*

Louise Stroud Murray '55 HEc

Buttermilk is a low-fat dairy product that you can make. Mix 1 teaspoon lemon juice or vinegar with 1 cup skim milk.

Penn State Magic Chocolate Cake

PREPARATION TIME: *50 minutes*
YIELD: *1 cake*

2 cups white flour

2 cups sugar

¾ cup cocoa

2 teaspoons baking soda

1 teaspoon baking powder

½ teaspoon salt

2 eggs

1 cup black coffee

1 cup milk

½ cup salad oil

2 teaspoons vanilla

1. Sift all dry ingredients together into a large bowl.

2. Add eggs and liquids, beat until batter is smooth. (Batter will be thin.)

3. Pour into a well-greased and floured 9 × 13-inch pan.

4. Place in center of oven. Bake at 350° for 35 minutes or until done. Cool in pan. Top with a favorite frosting.

"In our family, this is THE CAKE. It's a requirement for a birthday or a special event. This is a very moist, dark cake that becomes even more moist the second day. I always bake it the day before I plan to serve it."

Bonita (Bonnie) Koch Bleiler '74 EKEd

If decreasing caffeine is of interest, substitute a grain-based beverage, like Postum, for the coffee.

Chocolate Chip Carrot Cake

PREPARATION TIME: *10 minutes plus 1 hour baking time*
YIELD: *1 cake*

4 **eggs**	1. Combine eggs, sugar, and oil.
1 **cup sugar**	2. Sift together salt, flour, soda, baking powder, cinnamon, and add to egg mixture.
1 **cup salad oil**	
½ **teaspoon salt**	3. Add carrots and chocolate chips; mix well.
3 **cups flour**	
2 **teaspoons baking soda**	4. Place in greased round 9-inch tube pan.
2 **teaspoons baking powder**	
2 **teaspoons cinnamon**	5. Bake at 350° for one hour.
2 **(7 ounce) jars junior carrots (baby food)**	
12 **ounces chocolate chips**	

Due to the richness of this recipe a frosting is not required.

"I usually mix with a wooden spoon or fork; a beater isn't needed."

Angela Eichenmiller

United Parcel Service makes a daily stop at Ye Olde College Diner in State College to pick up packages of stickies to be shipped as far away as Hawaii, California and Texas. On a good day, 20-50 packages leave on the UPS truck.

Midnight Cake

PREPARATION TIME: *45 minutes*
YIELD: *1 three-layer cake*

1½	**cups sugar**
¾	**cup water**
1½	**cups cocoa**
1½	**teaspoons vanilla**
1⅛	**cups shortening**
1½	**cups sugar**
8	**eggs**
3	**cups flour**
¾	**teaspoon cinnamon**
1½	**tablespoons baking soda**
1½	**teaspoons salt**
1¾	**cups buttermilk**

1. In large bowl combine sugar, water, cocoa and vanilla. Stir until mixture is a thin paste.

2. Cream together shortening and 1½ cups sugar. Add paste mixture.

3. Add the eggs slowly.

4. Add flour, cinnamon, baking soda and salt; beat well.

5. Add buttermilk and mix batter well.

6. Pour into 3 greased 9-inch round cake pans.

7. Bake at 375° for 35 – 40 minutes.

8. Cool and frost with vanilla icing.

This recipe was and is a favorite of students and was printed in The Daily Collegian, *compliments of the campus bakery.*

Penn State Bakery

Penn State's bakery makes 27,389 meringue pies a year.

Undergrad Soft-Center Fudge Cake

PREPARATION TIME: *1 hour 20 minutes*
YIELD: *1 cake*

1¾ cups butter, softened

1¾ cups granulated sugar

6 eggs

2 cups powdered sugar

2¼ cups flour

¾ cup cocoa

1 teaspoon vanilla

2 cups chopped walnuts or
pecans

1. Grease and flour a 10-inch tube pan.

2. In large bowl beat together the butter and granulated sugar until light and fluffy.

3. Add eggs, one at a time, beating well after each addition.

4. Slowly add powdered sugar and blend well.

5. Stir in remaining ingredients by hand and blend well. Spoon batter into prepared pan.

6. Bake at 350° for 58 – 65 minutes.

7. Cool several hours before removing from pan. Best if completely cool before serving.

Since this cake has a soft fudgy interior an ordinary doneness test can not be used. An accurate oven temperature, the baking time and nuts are essential for the success and flavor of this cake.

"I was a senior living across from the old high school stadium on Nittany Avenue in a large house converted into a multi-unit apartment building when this cake became my first serious attempt at baking. My kitchen was 4 feet by 4 feet. In that space was a a sink, a refrigerator and two electric heating elements; no oven. I purchased a table-top oven big enough to cook a small turkey. However, its main function was to bake undergrad soft-center fudge cake."

Gerard F. Jackson '67 Zool

Great Grandma's Dutch Buttercake

PREPARATION TIME: *45 minutes*
YIELD: *24 – 28 squares*

1 **cup butter**

1 **cup sugar**

1 **egg**

2 **cups flour**

½ **cup almonds or walnuts**

1. Cream butter, add sugar and cream again.

2. Separate egg. Set white aside. Mix yolk into butter and sugar mixture.

3. Knead flour into butter mixture with well floured knuckles. (Add more flour as needed to handle, up to ½ cup more.)

4. Using your hand, press mixture flat in a 9 × 13-inch pan or 2 8-inch square pans. Flute edges with tines of fork.

5. Brush dough with egg white. Decorate with almonds or walnuts.

6. Bake at 350° for 35 minutes or until golden brown.

7. Let cool for 30 minutes before cutting into squares.

Rose (Ronnie) Schulman Saunders '45 Journ

Approximately 6,000 ice cream bars are sold each football game in Beaver Stadium.

Lemon Supreme Special Cake

PREPARATION TIME: *1 hour*
YIELD: *1 bundt cake*

1 2-layer lemon cake mix

½ cup sugar

4 eggs

½ cup salad oil

1 cup apricot nectar

1 cup powdered sugar

2 tablespoons lemon juice

1. In a large mixing bowl combine cake mix, sugar, eggs, oil and nectar. Mix until blended.

2. Beat at medium speed for 2 minutes.

3. Pour into a greased and floured bundt pan.

4. Bake at 350° for 45 – 55 minutes or until toothpick inserted in cake comes out clean.

5. Cool in pan for 25 minutes. Remove to wire rack to cool completely.

6. Stir together powdered sugar and lemon juice. Drizzle over cake.

James A. Leamer Jr. '51 AgEd

Penn State's bakery makes 45,000 fruit pies a year.

Business Logistics Pound Cake

PREPARATION TIME: *2 hours*
YIELD: *1 pound cake*

1 cup soft butter

3 cups sugar

6 eggs

½ teaspoon vanilla extract

¼ teaspoon almond extract

3 cups unsifted flour

½ pint heavy cream

1. Grease and flour a tube pan. Line bottom of pan with wax paper.

2. Cream butter and sugar together.

3. Add eggs, one at a time, beating well after each.

4. Add vanilla and almond extracts.

5. Alternately add cream and flour; mix well until thoroughly blended.

6. Pour batter into prepared pan and place in COLD OVEN.

7. Turn oven to 350° and bake for 30 minutes. After 30 minutes turn oven down to 325° and bake for 1 hour. (A total of 90 minutes.)

VARIATION: Mix some batter with melted chocolate and swirl through plain batter in tube pan.

"Served at department gatherings."

Joseph L. Cavinato '75 PhD BA

Strawberry Filled Angel Food Cake

PREPARATION TIME: *30 minutes plus 6 hours chilling time*
YIELD: *1 cake*

1 9- or 10-inch angel food cake (bake or buy)	
1 quart of ripe strawberries	
1 pint heavy cream	

1. Place the cake on a serving plate. Gently cut a 1-inch slice, crosswise, from top of cake; set aside. With knife, outline a cavity in cake, leaving 1½-inch thick walls. With a fork pull out the inside of the cake.

2. Crumble the removed inside of the cake into chunks.

3. Chop strawberries to make 2 cups.

4. Whip 1 cup of the heavy cream.

5. Gently fold together the cake chunks, strawberries and whipped cream.

6. Fill the cavity in the cake with the strawberry mixture. Replace the top section.

7. Whip the other cup of heavy cream and frost entire cake.

8. Refrigerate at least 6 hours.

"I usually fill the cake the night before it is to be served, then frost in the morning."

Harriet Wenner McGeehan '30 Ed

246

Nittany Lion Paw Cake

PREPARATION TIME: *20 minutes plus 24 hours chilling time*
YIELD: *12 – 15 servings*

DESSERT BASE

1 **(1 pound) box graham crackers**

2 **(3 ounce) boxes instant vanilla pudding**

3½ **cups milk**

1 **(9 ounce) container non-dairy whipped topping**

1. Butter bottom of a 9 × 13-inch pan and line with one-third of the graham crackers.

2. Mix pudding with milk.

3. Beat in whipped topping, using an electric mixer.

4. Pour half of this mixture over the graham crackers in the pan.

5. Place a second layer of crackers over pudding and pour remaining pudding mixture over this.

6. Cover with more crackers and refrigerate for 2 hours.

CHOCOLATE FROSTING

6 **tablespoons cocoa**

2 **tablespoons salad oil**

2 **teaspoons light corn syrup**

2 **teaspoons vanilla**

3 **tablespoons margarine, softened**

1½ **cups powdered sugar**

3 **tablespoons milk**

1. Blend all ingredients together in small mixing bowl.

2. Beat until smooth.

3. Spread over cake.

4. Refrigerate for 24 hours.

Blanche J. Metzgar '86 Nurs

Whole grain graham crackers without lard are available. Read labels to choose wisely.

Brewer Berry Special

PREPARATION TIME: *1 hour*
YIELD: *8 – 10 servings*

1 **cup miniature marshmallows**

2 **cups or 2 (10 ounce) packages frozen sliced strawberries in syrup, completely thawed**

1 **(3 ounce) package strawberry flavored gelatin**

2¼ **cups all-purpose flour**

1½ **cups sugar**

½ **cup shortening**

1 **tablespoon baking powder**

½ **teaspoon salt**

1 **cup milk**

1 **teaspoon vanilla**

3 **eggs**

1. Generously grease bottom only of 9 × 13-inch baking pan.

2. Sprinkle marshmallows evenly over bottom of pan.

3. Thoroughly combine strawberries and syrup with dry gelatin; set aside.

4. In large mixer bowl, combine flour, sugar, shortening, baking powder, salt, milk, vanilla and eggs. Blend at low speed until moistened.

5. Beat 3 minutes at medium speed, scraping sides of bowl occasionally.

6. Pour batter evenly over marshmallows in prepared pan.

7. Spoon strawberry mixture evenly over batter.

8. Bake at 350° for 45 – 50 minutes until golden brown.

9. Serve warm or cool with whipped cream or ice cream.

Elizabeth Brewer Lengle '81 MEd HEEd

College Avenue Cheesecake

PREPARATION TIME: *1 hour 15 minutes plus chilling time*
YIELD: *1 cake*

1½ **cups graham cracker crumbs**

4 **tablespoons melted butter**

4 **tablespoons sugar**

1 **pound cream cheese, softened**

½ **cup sugar**

1 **tablespoon lemon juice**

½ **teaspoon vanilla**

2 **eggs, separated**

TOPPING

1 **cup thick sour cream**

1 **teaspoon vanilla**

2 **tablespoons sugar**

1. Mix together by hand, graham cracker crumbs, melted butter, and 4 tablespoons sugar. Press mixture into a 9 × 3-inch springform pan.

2. Using electric mixer, blend cream cheese, ½ cup sugar, juice, and vanilla.

3. Add egg yolks, one at a time, beat well after each addition.

4. Beat egg whites until stiff; fold into mixture by hand. Pour over crumb base.

5. Bake at 300° for 50 minutes.

1. Mix sugar and vanilla into sour cream. Spread over top of cake and bake another 10 minutes. (Top will be tacky when done).

2. Remove from oven and cool on wire rack for one hour, then refrigerate. Serve when cool.

"I remember the Tavern for its wonderful cheesecake. This recipe is the closest I've come to matching its recipe."

Laura Danser Jackson '77 MedT

Orange County Club Cheesecake

PREPARATION TIME: *2 hours plus 3 hours chilling time*
YIELD: *1 cheese cake*

24 ounces cream cheese

1 cup plus 2 tablespoons sugar

2 tablespoons vanilla

5 eggs

1 pint sour cream

1 tablespoon sugar

1. Grease and flour a 9 × 3-inch spring-form pan.

2. In medium bowl, combine cream cheese, sugar, vanilla and eggs; beat until creamy. Pour batter into pan.

3. Bake at 350° for 1 hour. Let cool 20 minutes.

4. Mix sour cream and 1 tablespoon of sugar together; pour into the cavity on top which forms as cake cools for 20 minutes.

5. Return to oven for 10 minutes.

6. Refrigerate for 3 hours or overnight.

Spoon cherries, blueberries, boysenberries or your favorite fruit on top of cool cheesecake.

Richard W. Jantzer '63 Mgmt

Pumpkin Cheesecake

PREPARATION TIME: *2 hours*

YIELD: *1 cheesecake*

⅓ cup ground graham crackers

2 tablespoons melted butter

2 (8 ounce) packages cream cheese, softened

¾ cup sugar

2 eggs

⅛ cup flour

⅛ teaspoon salt

1½ cups pumpkin

1 teaspoon pumpkin pie spice

½ teaspoon cinnamon

¼ teaspoon ginger

⅛ teaspoon nutmeg

⅛ teaspoon cloves

1. Mix graham crackers and melted butter. Form a crust in bottom of a 9-inch pie pan.

2. Beat softened cream cheese and sugar together.

3. Add eggs, one at a time, mix well after each addition.

4. Add flour, salt, pumpkin and spices. Beat well.

5. Pour into prepared pie crust.

6. Bake at 325° for 1 hour and 15 minutes or until firm. (Up to 1 hour 30 minutes.)

7. Turn off oven, open door and let cool in oven for 30 minutes.

Margaret (Peggy) A. Costello '74 Psy

Try "yogurt cheese" instead of the cream cheese. Use a coffee filter cone, add yogurt and let set over a mug in the refrigerator until the liquid has filtered through, about 24 hours.

Mini Cheesecakes

PREPARATION TIME: *30 minutes plus 20 minutes baking time*
YIELD: *40 cheese cakes*

2 (8 ounce) packages cream cheese, softened

2 eggs

3 teaspoons vanilla

½ cup sugar

1 teaspoon lemon rind

40 vanilla wafers

Blueberry pie filling

1. Beat cream cheese and eggs until smooth.

2. Add vanilla, sugar and lemon rind. Mix well.

3. Place 1 small vanilla wafer in a small foil muffin tin.

4. Fill ¾ full with cream cheese mixture.

5. Place foil muffin tins on cookie sheet.

6. Bake at 350° for 18 minutes.

7. Place a tablespoon of blueberry pie filling on each and refrigerate.

Bertha Koelzer

For the Glory Pie

PREPARATION TIME: *1 hour*
YIELD: *1 pie*

¾ **cup sugar**

1 **cup sour cream**

3 **tablespoons flour**

¼ **teaspoon salt**

4 **cups blackberries**

¼ **cup fine bread crumbs**

2 **tablespoons sugar**

1 **tablespoon butter, melted**

1 **9-inch unbaked pie shell, or 9-inch graham cracker pie shell**

1. Combine ¾ cup sugar, sour cream, flour and salt. Set aside.

2. Place berries in pastry shell. Spread sour cream mixture over berries.

3. Combine bread crumbs, 2 tablespoons sugar and butter. Sprinkle on top of pie.

4. Bake at 375° for 40 – 45 minutes.

"Makes a nice blue and white colored pie."

Huberta Young Manning '58 HEc

Non-fat plain yogurt substitutes well for the sour cream or whip a cup of low-fat cottage cheese with 2 tablespoons skim milk and 1 tablespoon lemon juice.

Carrot Pie

PREPARATION TIME: *1 hour*
YIELD: *1 pie*

1 **cup grated raw carrots**

½ **cup cream (or evaporated milk, undiluted)**

1 **cup milk**

⅔ **cup sugar**

3 **eggs**

½ **teaspoon salt**

1 **teaspoon cinnamon**

¼ **teaspoon ginger**

1 **unbaked 9-inch pie shell**

1. Beat carrots, cream, milk, sugar, eggs, salt, cinnamon, and ginger together.

2. Pour into unbaked pie shell.

3. Bake at 425° for 10 minutes.

4. Reduce heat to 350° and bake for 30 minutes or until knife inserted in center comes out clean.

Gwendolyn B. Logan
John S. Logan '56 ME

Try skim evaporated milk and skim milk to decrease the fat. Egg whites (2 for 1) could be substituted for the eggs.

Peanut Butter-Cream Cheese Pie

PREPARATION TIME: *15 minutes plus 5 – 6 hours chilling time*
YIELD: *1 pie*

2 (3 ounce) packages cream cheese, softened

¾ cup sifted powdered sugar

½ cup peanut butter

2 tablespoons milk

1 (1.4 ounce) envelope dessert topping mix

1 8-inch graham cracker pie shell

Coarsely chopped peanuts

1. In small mixer bowl, beat together cream cheese and sugar until light and fluffy.

2. Add peanut butter and milk, beat until smooth and creamy.

3. Prepare dessert topping mix according to package directions; fold into peanut butter mixture.

4. Turn into prepared crust. Chill 5 – 6 hours or overnight.

5. Garnish with chopped peanuts.

Violet Carver Murphy '58 MEd BusEd

Lion's Paw Pecan Pie

PREPARATION TIME: *15 minutes plus 40 minutes baking time*
YIELD: *1 pie*

3 eggs, slightly beaten

1 cup Karo syrup

⅛ teaspoon salt

1 cup sugar

1 teaspoon vanilla

1 cup pecan meats

1 8- or 9-inch unbaked pastry pie shell

Whipped cream for garnish

1. Combine eggs, syrup, salt, sugar and vanilla together.

2. Add nuts and mix.

3. Pour mixture into pie shell.

4. Bake at 450° for 10 minutes, then reduce heat to 350°and continue baking until knife inserted in center comes out clean (about 30 minutes).

"Lion's Paw met regularly at the President's house and I always served this to the boys."

Josephine Schmeiser Walker '86 Honorary Alumna

Penn State's bakery makes 85,000 pies a year.

Shoo-Fly Pie

PREPARATION TIME: *1 hour 20 minutes*
YIELD: *1 pie*

1 **cup flour**

¾ **cup brown sugar**

1 **tablespoon margarine**

1 **teaspoon baking soda**

¾ **cup water**

1 **cup table molasses (dark Karo)**

1 **egg**

1 **10-inch unbaked pie crust**

1. In large bowl, mix flour, brown sugar and margarine with pastry blender to make crumbs. Set aside ½ cup crumbs.

2. Dissolve the baking soda in the water.

3. Mix together the water, molasses and egg. Add to the crumb mixture to make the pie filling.

4. Spread one tablespoon of the set aside crumbs in the bottom of the pie crust.

5. Add the filling. Sprinkle the remaining crumbs on top of the filling.

6. Bake at 400° for 15 minutes, reduce heat to 350° and bake for an additional 35 minutes.

"My grandmother gave me this recipe for wet-bottom shoo-fly pie. These pies have been excellent fund raisers; we've sold them at our local alumni club's bake sale to make money for our scholarship fund. Since shoo-fly pie is seldom seen in our location, it sells well, and it is fairly inexpensive to make."

Lenore Kreiser Holt '80 AmSt

Using dark molasses puts more iron in your diet. Try molasses instead of honey or other sweeteners in homemade breads.

257

Toll House Pie

PREPARATION TIME: *1 hour 15 minutes*
YIELD: *1 9-inch pie*

2 **eggs**	1. In medium mixing bowl beat eggs until foamy.
½ **cup flour**	
½ **cup sugar**	2. Beat in flour and sugars until well blended.
½ **cup packed brown sugar**	
1 **cup butter, melted and cooled to room temperature**	3. Blend in melted butter.
	4. Stir in chocolate chips and walnuts.
1 **cup chocolate chips**	5. Pour into pie shell.
1 **cup chopped walnuts**	6. Bake at 325° for 1 hour.
1 **9-inch unbaked pie shell**	7. Serve warm. Top with ice cream or whipped cream.

Suzanne Pohland Paterno '61 A&L

Desserts are usually high in cholesterol. To reduce the cholesterol substitute 2 egg whites for 1 egg.

Cranberry Pudding

PREPARATION TIME: *2½ hours*
YIELD: *8 – 10 servings*

PUDDING

½ **cup light molasses**

2 **teaspoons baking soda**

½ **cup hot water**

1½ **cups flour**

1 **pound fresh cranberries, each cut in half**

SAUCE

¾ **cup butter**

1½ **cups sugar**

¾ **cup whipping cream**

1½ **teaspoons vanilla**

1. Mix molasses, baking soda, water and flour in top of a double boiler.

2. Add cranberries. Mix well.

3. Cover and steam for 2 hours or longer.

4. Serve hot with a generous spoonful of sauce.

1. Blend butter and sugar in sauce pan and heat. Be very careful not to boil.

2. Add cream and vanilla; stir until blended.

Carole Ruff Merkel '58

To save time whirl cranberries briefly in your food processor with a little of the flour. Using part whole wheat flour will add to the nutrients.

PSU-Style Fudge Pudding

PREPARATION TIME: *1 hour 30 minutes*
YIELD: *6 – 8 servings*

⅞ cup brown sugar

½ cup granulated sugar

4½ tablespoons cocoa

1½ cups flour

2½ teaspoons baking powder

1¼ teaspoons salt

¾ cup sugar

2¾ tablespoons cocoa

2 tablespoons powdered milk

⅝ cup water

3 tablespoons melted shortening

½ teaspoon vanilla

⅜ cup chopped nuts

1¾ cups hot water

1. In mixing bowl, combine brown sugar, granulated sugar and cocoa. Mix by hand until blended and free of lumps. Set aside.

2. In separate mixing bowl, combine flour, baking powder, salt, sugar, cocoa, and milk and mix until blended and free of lumps.

3. Add remaining ingredients, except hot water, and mix until moist and smooth.

4. Pour batter into a 1½-quart greased pan.

5. Sprinkle dry ingredients, which you had set aside, over the batter. Pour 1¾ cups hot water over top.

6. Bake at 350° for 50 – 60 minutes.

"This recipe was served in the PSU dormitory cafeterias in the late 1970s. It was printed in The Daily Collegian. *The calorie count was out of this world, definitely not a 'diet item'."*

Kimberly S. Seman '81 Biol

Nittany Chocolate Bread Pudding

PREPARATION TIME: *1 hour 30 minutes*
YIELD: *4 – 6 servings*

2 cups milk	1. In a medium saucepan scald milk with sugar. Add cocoa and mix well.
¾ cup sugar	
3 heaping teaspoons cocoa	2. Add eggs to milk mixture and mix together.
2 eggs, beaten	
¼ teaspoon salt	3. Stir in salt, bread and vanilla.
4 slices stale bread, crust removed and cut in 1-inch squares	4. Pour into a 1-quart casserole dish and place in a pan of warm water.
½ teaspoon vanilla	5. Bake at 300° for 45 – 60 minutes.

June Daniels Mohan '45 A&L

Try skim milk and whole grain bread in this recipe to decrease fat and increase fiber.

Cajun Bread Pudding

PREPARATION TIME: *2 hours*
YIELD: *15 – 18 servings*

7 tablespoons unsalted butter, melted

¼ cup unsalted butter, melted

16 cups lightly packed, very dry French bread cubes (about 1 pound)

3 eggs

1½ cups sugar

2 tablespoons vanilla extract

1 teaspoon freshly grated nutmeg

3 cups milk

1½ teaspoons ground cinnamon

¾ cup golden raisins

¾ cup flaked coconut

½ cup coarsely chopped toasted pecans

1. Pour the 7 tablespoons butter into a 9 × 13-inch baking pan. Swirl butter around to coat bottom and sides. Pour excess butter and the additional ¼ cup butter into small bowl; set aside.

2. Place bread cubes in buttered baking dish; set aside.

3. In a large bowl, beat eggs and sugar with an electric mixer until thickened and light lemon colored, 3 – 4 minutes.

4. Add vanilla, nutmeg, milk, cinnamon, raisins, coconut, pecans and reserved butter. Beat on low speed to combine.

5. Pour liquid over bread in baking dish; stir to distribute nuts, coconut and raisins evenly. Set pan aside until bread has absorbed all of the liquid, 30 – 35 minutes. Press bread down into liquid often to cover all cubes with liquid.

6. Bake at 350° for 45 – 60 minutes, until crusty and golden brown. While baking, prepare rum sauce and soft cream.

7. When bread pudding has cooled to lukewarm, slice into squares. Place a spoonful of rum sauce in bottom of each serving bowl, add a square of bread pudding. Top with a generous dollop of cream.

RUM SAUCE

1 cup unsalted butter, room temperature

1½ cups sugar

2 large eggs, beaten until frothy

½ cup dark rum

1. Using an electric mixer, cream butter and sugar mixture until light and fluffy.

2. Put mixture in top of a double boiler over simmering water; cook 20 minutes, whisk often. The mixture should be silky smooth and light in color.

Continued on next page

3. Whisk 2 tablespoons hot butter mixture into beaten eggs, then 2 tablespoons more. Whisk warmed egg mixture slowly into remaining butter mixture.

4. Cook mixture over barely simmering water until mixture thickens, about 4 – 5 minutes, whisking constantly.

5. Cool slightly; whisk in rum. Sauce may be kept warm over hot water until served.

SOFT CREAM

2 **cups whipping cream**

⅓ **cup powdered sugar, sifted**

1 **tablespoon vanilla extract**

2 **tablespoons cognac or other brandy**

2 **tablespoons frangelico liqueur**

¼ **cup sour cream**

1. Chill beaters and bowl until very cold.

2. Place all ingredients in bowl; beat with an electric mixer on medium to high speed until soft, loose peaks form, about 3 – 4 minutes. The cream should have a slightly runny, cloud-like consistency that softly drapes over the bread pudding. Do not overbeat. Cover tightly and refrigerate until served.

William A. Dubas '85 EE

Nittany Bread Pudding Souffle

PREPARATION TIME: *1 hour 10 minutes*
YIELD: *8 servings*

½ cup milk	1. In a small bowl combine milk, amaretto, sugar, vanilla, salt, and dry bread cubes; mix and set aside.
¼ cup amaretto liqueur	
¼ cup sugar	
½ teaspoon vanilla	2. In a small saucepan melt butter, add flour, ⅛ teaspoon salt and milk; cook until thick.
⅛ teaspoon salt	
1½ cups dry bread cubes	
3 tablespoons butter	3. In a separate bowl beat egg yolks, stir in flour mixture, then stir in bread cube mixture.
¼ cup flour	
⅛ teaspoon salt	
¾ cup milk	4. In a large clean bowl beat egg whites until stiff; gradually add ¼ cup sugar and vanilla
4 egg yolks	
4 egg whites	5. Fold egg whites into bread mixture and turn into a 2-quart souffle dish with a 2-inch collar made of aluminum foil which has been buttered and sugared.
¼ cup sugar	
½ teaspoon vanilla	
	6. Bake at 325° for 50 – 55 minutes. Serve with Satiny Sauce.

SATINY SAUCE

½ cup butter	1. In small sauce pan melt butter and add sugar; cook until sugar dissolves.
¾ cup sugar	
1 egg, beaten	2. Add a small amount to one beaten egg and mix. Stir into remaining sauce and cook 2 minutes.
¼ cup amaretto	
	3. Stir in amaretto and serve warm.

Must serve immediately.

Elissa M. Sichi
Harry J. Sichi '59 A&L

264

Lion's Claw Tarts

PREPARATION TIME: *1 hour*
YIELD: *12 servings*

SHELLS

6 tablespoons butter

¼ cup sugar

1 cup sifted flour

¼ teaspoon almond flavoring (optional)

1. Cream butter, gradually add sugar, then blend in flour. Add almond flavoring if desired.

2. Divide dough into 12 ungreased mini muffin tins.

3. Press firmly around the sides and halfway up.

4. Bake at 350° for 10 minutes.

FILLING

⅓ cup slivered almonds

¼ cup sugar

2 tablespoons butter

1½ tablespoons cream

2 teaspoons flour

1. Combine all filling ingredients and cook quickly, stirring constantly, until it boils.

2. Pour filling into the pastry shells.

3. Bake at 350° for 10 – 15 minutes.

4. Cool a few minutes before removing from the pan.

Virginia Minshall Swartz '47 Ed, '51 MEd Engl, '85 PhD SpCom

Nittany Lion Lemon Squares

PREPARATION TIME: *1 hour*

YIELD: *16 – 20 squares*

1 cup flour

½ cup butter

¼ cup powdered sugar

2 eggs

1 cup sugar

½ teaspoon baking powder

2½ tablespoons fresh lemon juice

Dash of salt

Powdered sugar

1. Blend together flour, butter and powdered sugar with fingertips until well mixed. Grease bottom of an 8 × 8-inch square baking pan, pat in flour mixture.

2. Bake at 350° for 20 minutes.

3. While crust is baking combine remaining ingredients and beat together by hand. Pour over baked crust and return to oven for 20 – 25 minutes. Cool in pan on wire rack and sprinkle with powdered sugar. Cut into squares.

Diane Freiermuth Travers '84 AdmJ

Apple Dumplings

PREPARATION TIME: *1 hour 10 minutes*
YIELD: *6 dumplings*

PASTRY

2¼ cups sifted flour

¾ teaspoon salt

¾ cup shortening

7 – 8 tablespoons ice water

1. Sift flour and salt into mixing bowl.

2. Add shortening and cut in with a pastry blender until mixture is in even bits about the size of peas.

3. Sprinkle water lightly over mixture, blend with a fork until dough can be pressed lightly into a ball.

4. Divide dough into six evenly-sized balls. Roll out each piece of dough to a thickness of ⅛ inch when ready to put apples on dough.

APPLES AND FILLING

6 medium apples

½ cup sugar

1½ teaspoons cinnamon

1 tablespoon butter

1. Pare and core apples. Place one apple on each piece of rolled out pastry.

2. Mix sugar and cinnamon together.

3. Fill cavity of apples with the sugar and cinnamon mixture. Dot with some of the butter.

4. Moisten corners of rolled out pastry square. Bring opposite corners up over the apple, overlapping them. Seal well.

5. Place dumplings in an 8 × 12-inch baking pan. Chill thoroughly.

SYRUP

1 cup sugar

¼ teaspoon cinnamon

4 tablespoons butter

2 cups water

1. Mix these ingredients together in a saucepan. Boil for 3 minutes.

2. Pour the hot syrup around the chilled dumplings in the baking pan.

3. Bake immediately for 5 – 7 minutes at 500° until the crust shows slight coloring. Reduce temperature to 350°and bake about 30 – 35 minutes longer.

Serve warm with the hot syrup and with milk or cream, if desired.

"This favorite Breisch family recipe has been enjoyed by three generations of Penn Staters."

Phyllis Breisch Stuby '60 EKEd, '69 MEd CDFR

The Lion and the Mousse

PREPARATION TIME: *10 minutes plus 1 hour chilling time*

YIELD: *6 servings*

5 tablespoons boiling water	1. Place water and chocolate chips in blender. Blend at high speed for 10 seconds.
6 ounces chocolate chips	
4 egg yolks	2. Add egg yolks, cognac, cinnamon and coffee; blend for 10 seconds.
2 tablespoons cognac	
¼ teaspoon cinnamon (if desired)	3. Add egg whites; blend at low speed for one minute.
½ teaspoon instant coffee	
4 egg whites	4. Spoon mixture into 6 demitasse cups and refrigerate for at least 1 hour.

"Very rich; serve small portions. Whipped cream is a nice touch on top."

Phyllis S. Imber
Herman D. Imber '39 A&L

The Creamery's most popular flavor is vanilla, followed by chocolate. Butter pecan is third, with mint chocolate chip fourth.

Lion's Fantasy

PREPARATION TIME: *1 hour plus 3 days chilling time*
YIELD: *12 servings*

2 cups semi-sweet chocolate chips	1. Melt the chocolate chips over low heat.
1 cup butter, softened	2. Beat in the butter and sugar.
1 cup sugar	3. Add egg yolks and beat for 10 – 15 minutes.
8 egg yolks	
8 egg whites	4. In separate bowl beat egg whites until stiff.
Cool Whip	5. Fold whites into yolk mixture.
Chocolate curls	6. Pour ⅔ of the batter into a greased 10-inch springform pan.
	7. Bake at 325° for 30 minutes.
	8. Let stand until cake cools to room temperature. (Cake will fall.)
	9. Spread rest of batter over torte.
	10. Cover and refrigerate for 3 days.
	11. When ready to serve cover with Cool Whip and chocolate curls.

Jacquelyn Wengert Jenkins '49 PhEd

Trifle

PREPARATION TIME: *30 minutes*
YIELD: *14 – 16 servings*

1 (3½ ounce) package vanilla instant pudding

1 angel food cake

1 (11 ounce) can mandarin oranges

¼ cup rum

2 bananas, sliced

10 cherries, chopped

1 (8 ounce) can crushed pineapple

2 (8 ounce) containers non-dairy whipped topping

1. Prepare pudding according to package directions.

2. Cube cake; pour ¼ cup juice from the oranges and rum over cubes.

3. In a clear glass bowl alternate layers of cake, pudding, whipped topping, chopped cherries, crushed pineapple, sliced bananas and orange segments. Repeat layers.

4. Refrigerate until serving.

Can do ahead. Moderately easy.

Judith Reid Green '61 HEc

Lyons' Kahlua Brownies

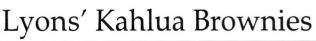

PREPARATION TIME: *20 minutes plus 30 minutes baking time*
YIELD: *1½ dozen*

3 eggs

2 cups sugar

⅔ cup butter or margarine

3 ounces baking chocolate

¼ cup Kahlua

1½ cups flour

Pinch salt

½ teaspoon baking powder

Extra Kahlua to brush on brownies

1. Cream eggs and sugar.

2. Melt butter and chocolate, add to creamed mixture.

3. Add Kahlua and mix well.

4. Stir in flour, salt and baking powder to mixture.

5. Pour into 9 × 13-inch pan.

6. Bake at 350° for 30 minutes.

7. Remove from oven and brush with extra Kahlua.

Anita E. Lyons

Sinful Brownies

PREPARATION TIME: *40 minutes*
YIELD: *24 – 30 brownies*

1 **cup butter or margarine**	1. Melt butter in saucepan, add cocoa, stir and remove from heat.
⅔ **cup cocoa**	
2 **cups sugar**	2. Stir in sugar, then eggs.
4 **eggs**	3. Add flour and stir by hand until blended. Pour into an ungreased 9 × 13-inch pan.
1½ **cups flour**	
	4. Bake at 350° for 20 minutes.
	5. Frost while hot.

FROSTING

4 **tablespoons soft butter or margarine**	1. Melt the butter, then blend in cocoa. Stir in vanilla and sugar.
3 **tablespoons cocoa**	2. Add milk and stir until consistency is spreadable. Frost. Cool and cut into squares.
2 **teaspoons vanilla**	
2 **cups powdered sugar**	
2 – 3 **tablespoons milk**	

Sandra Murdock Greene '66 SoW

271

Peanut Butter Fudge Brownies

PREPARATION TIME: *45 minutes*
YIELD: *24 large brownies*

BROWNIE

1 (21.5 ounce) box brownie mix

½ cup very hot water

½ cup salad oil

2 eggs

1. In a large bowl, combine box of dry brownie mix, hot water, oil and eggs. Beat 50 strokes by hand.

2. Grease the bottom only of a 9 × 13-inch pan. Spread batter in pan.

3. Bake at 350° for 30 minutes. Immediately upon taking brownies out of oven start to prepare fudge so you can spread it on while both are hot.

FUDGE

2¾ cups sugar

½ cup margarine

1 (5⅓ ounce) can evaporated milk

1¼ cups creamy peanut butter

1 (7 ounce) jar marshmallow creme

1 teaspoon vanilla

6 ounces semi-sweet chocolate chips (optional)

1. Using a 3-quart sauce pan, combine sugar, margarine and evaporated milk. Bring to a full rolling boil, stirring constantly. Continue to boil for 5 minutes over medium heat or until candy thermometer reaches 234°; stir constantly to prevent scorching.

2. Remove from heat and stir in peanut butter until melted.

3. Add marshmallow creme and vanilla, beat by hand until well blended. Pour immediately onto brownies in pan and smooth out to edges.

VARIATION: Sprinkle with chocolate chips, let stand 5 minutes, then cut through with a knife for a marble effect.

"I was threatened with eviction from a tailgate party one weekend when I hadn't brought these along."

Bette A. Bender '77 EKEd

272

Peanut Butter-Chocolate Chip Bars

PREPARATION TIME: *30 minutes*
YIELD: *8 large bars*

1 box 2-layer yellow or white cake mix

¾ cup water

2 eggs

4 tablespoons softened margarine

1 cup crunchy peanut butter

12 ounces chocolate chips

1. Pour half of the cake mix into a bowl. Add water, eggs, margarine, and peanut butter. Mix until smooth.

2. Blend in chocolate chips and remaining cake mix. Dough will be very stiff.

3. Spread mixture evenly in an ungreased 9 × 13-inch pan.

4. Bake at 375° for 20 minutes, until puffed, set, and golden.

5. Cut into squares (Penn State size, 2 × 4 inches).

VARIATION: Use butterscotch chips with yellow cake mix, peanut butter chips with chocolate cake mix or try half chocolate chips and half butterscotch chips with yellow cake mix.

Penn State Food Service

Mock Pralines

PREPARATION TIME: *30 minutes*

YIELD: *75 – 85 pieces*

22 double graham crackers, (or more if needed to line pan)	1. Line an 11½ × 17-inch jelly roll pan with whole graham crackers.
1 cup margarine	2. Melt margarine over low heat, add brown sugar and boil together for one minute.
1 cup brown sugar	
1½ cups broken pecans	3. Add pecans to syrup. Pour syrup mixture over crackers, spreading pecans as needed.
	4. Bake at 350° for 10 minutes.
	5. Cool in pan, then break into uneven pieces.

Best if allowed to stand overnight.

Rosella (Suzy) Katz Fenton '49 Aersp

274

Mint Nittany Cookies

PREPARATION TIME: *45 minutes*
YIELD: *72 cookies*

¾ **cup butter**

1½ **cups brown sugar**

2 **tablespoons water**

12 **ounces chocolate chips**

2 **eggs**

2½ **cups flour**

1¼ **teaspoons baking soda**

½ **teaspoon salt**

2 **(6 ounce) boxes Andes Cream de Menthe Candies, unwrapped**

1. In 2-quart saucepan over low heat, cook butter, brown sugar, and water until melted.

2. Add chocolate chips. Heat until partially melted. Remove from heat and stir until chocolate is completely melted. Pour this mixture into large mixing bowl and let stand for 10 minutes.

3. With mixer at high speed, add eggs to the slightly cooled mixture. Reduce speed to low and add dry ingredients.

4. Line cookie sheet with foil. Drop dough 2 inches apart on cookie sheet.

5. Bake at 350° for 12 – 13 minutes. Remove from oven immediately.

6. Place 1 mint on each cookie. After a few seconds swirl the mint with your finger. Cool and remove from sheet.

Marjorie Ganter Scholtz '62 A&L

Penn State's bakery makes 110,000 dozen cookies a year.

Nittany Lion Molasses Cookies

PREPARATION TIME: *1 hour plus overnight chilling*
YIELD: *4 dozen*

1 cup brown sugar

1 cup dark molasses

1 cup margarine or shortening

1 cup buttermilk

2 eggs

4 – 5 cups flour

3 teaspoons baking soda

1 teaspoon cinnamon

¼ teaspoon nutmeg

¼ teaspoon ginger

¼ teaspoon ground cloves

Sugar, for tops of cookies

1. In a large bowl combine brown sugar, molasses and margarine; beat well.

2. Add buttermilk and eggs, mixing well.

3. Sift flour, soda, and spices together. Gradually add to margarine mixture. Chill stiff dough overnight.

4. On lightly floured surface, roll dough, one part at a time, ½ inch thick. With floured cookie cutter, cut out cookies.

5. Place cookies on cookie sheets, sprinkle with sugar,

6. Bake at 400° for 8 – 10 minutes.

"This recipe makes excellent gingerbread lions. Put a hole in top before baking so you can hang them on the tree with blue and white ribbons and have a wonderful Nittany Lion Christmas!"

Kathie Martin

Mom Stufft's Toll House Cookies

PREPARATION TIME: *45 minutes*

YIELD: *4 dozen*

1 cup shortening	1. With electric mixer cream shortening.
¾ cup brown sugar	2. Gradually add sugar, cream until light and fluffy.
¾ cup white sugar	
2 eggs	3. Add eggs, one at a time, mix well after each addition.
1 teaspoon hot water	4. Add hot water and mix well.
1½ cups sifted flour	5. Combine flour, soda and salt together. Add to mixture along with vanilla.
1 teaspoon baking soda	
1 teaspoon salt	
2 teaspoons vanilla	6. Stir in nuts, chocolate chips, and oatmeal.
1 cup chopped walnuts	7. Drop by teaspoonfuls on cookie sheets.
12 ounces chocolate chips	
2 cups oatmeal (quick cooking oats)	8. Bake at 375° for 12 – 15 minutes.

Ruth Stufft Van Akin '54 MuEd
Gerald R. Van Akin '55 ABCh

A coed writes how she baked cookies in the dorms: "I would put two irons on the floor, holding them up with sneakers. I would put a piece of aluminum foil over the irons so no cookie dough would fall into the iron holes. Plus, I would always use that pre-packaged freezer-style dough for convenience sake.

For almost an entire year, my iron cookies were a joy to create and fun for the other girls on the floor, detecting a chocolate-chip aroma from the end of the hall."

Rah Rah Rogelach

PREPARATION TIME: *1 hour plus at least 2 hours chilling time*

YIELD: *4 – 5 dozen*

8 ounces cream cheese

1 cup butter

1¾ cups flour

8 tablespoons sugar

1 egg white

Filling: any good quality preserves (strawberry, apricot, raspberry) or a mixture of chopped walnuts, sugar and cinnamon

1. Let cream cheese and butter soften to room temperature.

2. Work butter into cream cheese with fork.

3. Add flour and sugar. Knead into a sticky dough.

4. Cover and place in refrigerator for 2 hours or overnight.

5. Flour board and rolling pin. Divide dough into 4 parts. Roll out one section. Using a square cookie cutter (about 2-inch square), cut squares.

6. Fill each square with a dab of filling. Fold opposite corners into center. Seal with a little egg white.

7. Place on greased cookie sheet.

8. Bake at 350° for 20 minutes or until light brown.

Judith Kaplan Anchel
Edward Anchel '60 BA

Little Lion Shoo Flies

PREPARATION TIME: *1 hour plus 1 hour chilling time*
YIELD: *30 cookies/mini pies*

CRUST

1 cup flour

½ cup butter

3 ounces cream cheese

1. Mix flour, butter and cream cheese well. Chill for 1 hour.

2. Form into 30 balls and shape with fingers into mini muffin tins.

FILLING

1 egg

¾ cup brown sugar, packed

1 teaspoon vanilla

1 tablespoon milk

1. Mix together filling ingredients until a syrup is formed.

2. Place ¾ teaspoon syrup into each shell.

CRUMB TOPPING

¼ cup butter

½ cup sugar

¾ cup flour

1. Mix crumb topping together. Use a teaspoon to fill each shell to the top.

2. Bake at 400° for 15 – 20 minutes.

Lisa K. Pollisino '85 FSer

The Creamery produces 20,000 pounds of cream cheese and sour cream a year.

Zucchini Bars with Caramel Frosting

PREPARATION TIME: *1 hour plus 30 minutes cooling time*

YIELD: *24 – 36 bars*

BARS

3 cups flour

1½ teaspoons baking soda

1 teaspoon baking powder

1 teaspoon salt

⅛ teaspoon nutmeg

⅛ teaspoon cloves

¾ cup margarine

1 cup brown sugar

½ cup sugar

1 teaspoon vanilla

2 eggs

2 cups peeled and grated zucchini

½ cup butterscotch chips

1. Sift together flour, baking soda, baking powder, salt, nutmeg and cloves.

2. In a separate bowl, cream together margarine, brown sugar, sugar, vanilla and eggs. Combine flour mixture and butter mixture by hand.

3. Gradually add zucchini and butterscotch chips. Pour into a greased and floured 9 × 13-inch pan.

4. Bake at 375° for 30 – 35 minutes. Cool for 30 minutes then frost with caramel frosting.

CARAMEL FROSTING

½ cup margarine

1 cup brown sugar

¼ cup milk

1 – 1½ cups powdered sugar

1. In medium saucepan over low heat melt margarine. Add brown sugar and bring to boil for 2 minutes.

2. Add milk and bring to second boil. Remove from heat.

3. Add enough powdered sugar so frosting spreads easily.

Debra K. Young '86 EKEd

Good Bars

PREPARATION TIME: *30 minutes*
YIELD: *24 bars*

2 **cups flour**

1 **cup brown sugar**

1 **cup granulated sugar**

1 **cup oatmeal**

1 **cup walnuts or pecans**

1 **cup chocolate chips**

1 **teaspoon salt**

1 **teaspoon baking powder**

1 **teaspoon baking soda**

3 **eggs, beaten**

1 **cup salad oil**

1. With a large spoon mix ingredients together in order given.

2. Spread in an ungreased $18 \times 12 \times 1$-inch pan.

3. Bake at 350° for 18 – 20 minutes. Do not overbake.

4. Cut into squares immediately after removing from oven, then let cool in pan.

Carolyn Spengler Tothero '55 HEc

Oatmeal and oat bran have cholesterol-lowering properties. Use them often!

Mt. Nittany Mud

PREPARATION TIME: *1 hour*

YIELD: *24 – 36 squares*

1 cup margarine

½ cup cocoa

2 cups sugar

4 eggs, slightly beaten

1½ cups flour

Pinch of salt

1 teaspoon vanilla

1½ cups chopped nuts

1 small package miniature marshmallows

1. Melt margarine and cocoa together.

2. Add sugar, eggs, flour, salt, vanilla and nuts. Stir well by hand. Pour into a greased 9 × 13-inch pan.

3. Bake at 350° for 35 – 40 minutes. It will be moist in the center.

4. Remove from oven and immediately cover top with marshmallows.

5. Pour topping over cake while hot.

TOPPING

½ cup margarine

½ cup cocoa

½ cup milk

1 pound powdered sugar

1. Melt margarine, cocoa and milk together. Stir in sugar until smooth, pour over cake while hot. Cool and cut into squares.

Anne Curry Piper '52

Love Ya Lion Fudge

PREPARATION TIME: *30 minutes plus 1 hour chilling time*
YIELD: *50 pieces*

1 **pound powdered sugar**

1 **cup butter, melted**

8 **ounces peanut butter**

4 **tablespoons cocoa**

1 **tablespoon vanilla**

1 **cup chopped walnuts (optional)**

1. In a large bowl slowly blend sugar with melted butter. Stir by hand until well blended.

2. Add peanut butter, cocoa, vanilla and walnuts if desired. Mix until all ingredients are well blended.

3. Press into a greased 8 × 12-inch pan or dish, using wax paper to press evenly in pan.

4. Place in refrigerator until firm (at least 1 hour). Cut into squares and serve.

Diane K. Wendling '84 Art

Raspberry Truffles

PREPARATION TIME: *1 hour 30 minutes*
YIELD: *3 dozen*

8 **ounces chocolate sandwich cookies**

3 **ounces unsweetened chocolate**

⅓ **cup softened butter**

1¼ **cups powdered sugar**

3 **large egg yolks**

1 **teaspoon Chambord liqueur**

1. Crumb cookies in blender, set aside.

2. Melt chocolate over double boiler.

3. Combine butter and powdered sugar, blend well.

4. Beat egg yolks into butter-sugar mixture one at a time.

5. Stir in chocolate and Chambord liqueur.

6. Chill mixture, shape into ½-inch balls, roll in cookie crumbs. Store in airtight container in cool, dry place or refrigerate.

Maryellen B. Cannon '72 EKEd

Lion Whiskers

PREPARATION TIME: *10 minutes*
YIELD: *15 – 20 servings*

1 **pound white chocolate**

2 **cups stick pretzels, broken slightly**

8 **ounces unsalted dry-roasted peanuts**

1. Melt chocolate in double boiler or in microwave.

2. Combine pretzels and peanuts in large bowl.

3. Pour melted chocolate over pretzels and peanuts. Toss quickly and pour onto large tray covered with wax paper. Spread mixture out as thinly as you can.

4. Refrigerate for 5 minutes. Break candy into pieces and enjoy.

Can use morsels or caps of chocolate that are green or pink.

Janet Woolever Raytek '65 FSHA
James J. Raytek '65, '67 MS FSHA

Lion Butter

PREPARATION TIME: *25 minutes plus chilling time*
YIELD: *40 squares*

1 pound white chocolate (I use ½ pound Nestles Alpine white and ½ pound plain white chocolate morsels.)

12 ounces chunky peanut butter

1 pound chocolate (½ pound milk chocolate and ½ pound semi-sweet), melted

1. Combine white chocolate and peanut butter in top of double boiler. Bring water to boil.

2. Reduce heat to low and cook until chocolate and peanut butter melt, stirring constantly.

3. Spread mixture onto a wax paper lined 9 × 13-inch pan.

4. Pour melted chocolate (milk chocolate/semi-sweet) over the peanut butter mixture.

5. Swirl through both mixtures with a knife.

6. Chill until firm. Cut into squares. Store in refrigerator.

Lori Bowers Uhazie '82 Advt

Canteen food services sell around 2,000 boxes of candy in Beaver Stadium each football game.

Index

C

290

293

298

NOTES:

NOTES:

NOTES:

NOTES:

NOTES:

NOTES: